BODY OF WORK

"The internet can scale just about anything, but it can't scale the intimacy of exploring an artist's body of work, and the album's resilience is captured in this remarkable book."

Will Page, author of *Tarzan Economics*

"Is the album dead? It isn't and it is. We can therefore approach **Body of Work** *as a thought experiment: let's call it Schrödinger's catalogue. Jopling explores why the album is the historical anomaly that battled through multiple format shifts to (mostly) endure artistically, culturally, and economically.* **Body of Work** *is part eulogy for the album's past glories and part electioneering for the album's future relevance."*

Eamonn Forde, author of *The Final Days of EMI*

"Why does the album endure in the streaming age? Keith Jopling's neat treatise on the album as an artistic format provides the answer, taking in the history of the album, the technological changes of the music industry, the artistic drive that the LP format fulfils, and some personal reflections along the way. A clear-headed summation of the album's evergreen appeal."

Will Hodgkinson, Chief Rock and Pop Critic, *The Times*

"Keith Jopling, at once advocate and analyst, has written an affectionate and insightful account of the album's survival in a hostile age of streaming and algorithms."

Ludo Hunter-Tilney, Arts and Pop Critic, *FT*

"This book made me fall in love with the art of the album again, and I'm sure it will do the same for you. A must read for any true music fan."

Shain Shapiro, author of *This Must Be the Place*

BODY OF WORK

How the album outplayed the algorithm and survived playlist culture

Keith Jopling

Published by Repeater Books

An imprint of Watkins Media Ltd

Unit 11 Shepperton House

89-93 Shepperton Road

London

N1 3DF

United Kingdom

www.repeaterbooks.com

A Repeater Books paperback original 2026

1

Distributed in the United States by Random House, Inc., New York.

ISBN: 9781917516334

Ebook ISBN: 9781917516341

Printed and bound by CPI Group (UK) Ltd, Croydon, CR0 4YY

This book is dedicated to Freddie Mercury, Queen, and all album artists before and since

Contents

Chapter	Page No.
Foreword: The album is still "God"	xi
Introduction: Going back to go forward, for the love of vinyl	1
Chapter 1: Spotify kills the album, almost	9
Chapter 2: An alternative/personal history of the album	18
Chapter 3: Digital music and the dismantling of the disc	39
Chapter 4: Record retail and the vinyl resurgence	70
Chapter 5: Music consumption in the song economy	80
Chapter 6: Classic albums then and now	91
Chapter 7: The future of the album	104
Afterword: Celebrating the album	125
"Fortress Album": Twenty-five titles that have helped the format survive the twenty-first century	125
Still hitting the heights: Great new albums by older bands	137
Further Reading and Resources: Vinyl aspirations and inspirations	139

Foreword

The album is still "God"

There have been relatively few books written about the album as an art form. Mostly, they relate to the resurgence of vinyl records — the perfect vessel for the album and true incarnation of the format. David Hepworth's *A Fabulous Creation* is 321 pages of brilliant homage to the vinyl L.P. and its glory years, 1967 through to 1982. I've read the book twice from cover to cover. The second time around, one brief statement made me stop and think. In fact, I took issue with it. On page 264, Hepworth states, with his usual level of confident, scholarly authority, that "art can't buck the market". By way of example, Hepworth explains how Charles Dickens originally released his famously epic novels in monthly instalments, since they were published as serialisations in *The Monthly Magazine*. In order to get his work published, the greatest storyteller of his time had to work within the limits of the popular format of the time.

But if art can't buck the market, what can? It occurred to me that the music album has indeed bucked the market. For five decades, the album *was* the music market, firstly during the analogue era of vinyl that began in the second half of the 1960s and (along with the cassette) ascended through the '70s and '80s. Then came the '90s CD boom and the transition to digital, during which time the album's prominence was never questioned. The CD bloated and then eventually devalued the album, but never challenged its relevance. It took the popularisation of the internet to do that. When Napster came along and atomised albums into a hundred million separate song files, the disruptive effect was too big for the music industry to handle, and it began to lose control of its most lucrative invention. The twenty-first century ushered in a different version of the music business — one whose tune was no longer called by an elite set of "music men" presiding over a feudal system, but by a cluster of "tech bros", with varying levels of indifference to music as an art form, but an insatiable appetite for music as "content" with which to feed their respective digital channels. Respect for the album took a hammering, and concluding that the "art can't buck the market" wasn't only logical but seemed like a foregone conclusion. First, Apple's iTunes unbundled it, with the music industry's blessing. The album wobbled but hung on. Then the juggernaut arrived. Spotify decided that the best way to kill the album was to ignore it altogether, putting playlists and songs first, while placing albums on automatic shuffle (until Adele stepped in and had a polite word). And look where we've gone from there. TikTok, Reels and Shorts have reduced the human attention span so much that these platforms have cut songs down into "clips", or even just sounds. Content creators consider anything lasting more than a minute to be "long form". Tossed into the mix, music marketers are caught in a spin, desperate to have their latest project included as a soundtrack to the daily tidal wave of social media posts.

Meanwhile, artists may tentatively ask, "How's my album doing?" As for the response from record labels, look away now. It's a miracle artists even got to make albums at all, but in the end, the format endured. It was never fully dismantled, but went through a series of extremely close calls, somehow resisting all attempts on its life. As of 2026, the album feels, in many ways, stronger than ever and getting stronger. Vinyl is back. Eight to twelve tracks per album is back. Sleeve notes are back. Cover art is back. The concept album is back. The *classic* album may even be back. This is good for artists and good for fans. And good for the music business once it realises fully what has happened here.

Jack Antonoff, one of the music world's most successful producers and collaborators, and a substantial musical artist in his own right (as Bleachers), already knows this. He recently expressed, in no uncertain terms, that "the album is God" (or rather, he expelled the myth in the music business that the album *isn't* God). As a cultural commentator, Antonoff is as confidently authoritative as David Hepworth, but as one of the industry's most successful current creators, he is inarguably more in tune with the underbelly of today's music business. Here is what he told *The Writer Is...* podcast in 2025: "The album is God. Period. There's no brilliant artist that hasn't existed for a real period of time and changed things and has a real audience that isn't based on albums. They don't exist."

Antonoff is not just looking back. His words speak very much of the music industry now. Artists aspire to see their work in the album format. Indeed, I've yet to come across an artist that doesn't appreciate albums and the idea of seeing their work come to life as an expression of this art form — a statement of where they are creatively at a point in time and a stage in their career and life. The opportunity to add to the legacy, the canon, the oeuvre. It is the purest package for the endeavour of making songs — to put them together as an album — *a body of work*.

Antonoff has worked closely with the biggest artist on Earth, and also the smartest music marketer of all, Taylor Swift, who undoubtedly sees herself as an "album artist".

In July 2020, at the height of the COVID-19 pandemic, Swift released her eighth studio album, *Folklore*. It was "dropped" without fanfare or any kind of campaign whatsoever. Swift recorded vocals in her home studio and worked virtually with the producers, Antonoff and Aaron Dessner, who also worked from their respective home studios. The album took both fans and critics — everyone, in fact — by surprise, not only because no one expected a new Taylor Swift album just then, but because the record was a stylistic departure from her previous catalogue, the clue being in the title: a stripped-back set of simple songs more akin to folk than pop or country. The album was successful on every level. It was a hit, but it also signalled Swift as an artist willing to take risks and look to new horizons musically, while at the same time relying on the understated simplicity of her own songwriting, singing and musicianship. Most of all, *Folklore* is an album with a clear concept and meaning in the streaming era. It's structured like a literary work, filled with interwoven characters, narratives and subtle references. It's an album in which the stream counts for all of the individual songs are relatively evenly distributed, which, these days, is unusual. Of course, some songs are bigger than others, but the ratio between the most streamed track ("Cardigan") and the least ("Hoax") is 7.4. That's remarkably low for such a massive artist in the 2020s. By dropping the album as a whole, Swift invited fans to play it right through (something that may also have made more sense to people in the middle of pandemic, when slowing down and paying more attention was easier), so it was for listeners to decide which songs were their favourites. No lead single. No appetiser and main course — just a high-quality buffet.

By dropping *Folklore* unexpectedly, Swift made the album release the start of something. It wasn't a campaign so much as a statement of intent: "I've made something. Here it is." It reversed the prevailing wisdom that, in the streaming era, the best way to hype an album is to cram as many bells and whistles as possible (including multiple singles) into a campaign leading up to the album itself. This being the best way to achieve a return on investment for what is an expensive thing to create, but which is essentially out of step with the world into which it is released. Of course, it doesn't work that way. Instead, albums quickly evaporate into the atmosphere and disappear into the vast musical ozone layer of streaming platforms.

Folklore was such a phenomenal success that Swift didn't stop there. She made another, similar but different album — a companion record some might say — *Evermore*, released the following year. Also a success (with an even lower song stream count differential of 6.9), this pair of albums seemed to lay a foundation from which Taylor Swift would climb to the very top of the music industry pedestal over the next few years, culminating in the highest-grossing tour in history, the *Eras* tour. This was not a foregone conclusion by any means. Taylor Swift's superstar reputation before the COVID-19 pandemic could have gone either way. With these two records, all previous doubters, of whom there were plenty, were won over. The country-pop sensation could turn her hand to folk. She could make a quietly understated full-length album that Swifties embraced and everyone else respected. And she did it twice.

In doing so, Swift became one of a select few artists who helped build "Fortress Album" — a modern day indestructible refuge for serious artists everywhere. They will lower the drawbridge for like-minded collaborators and a discernible audience of any age, but stressed-out music industry marketers, tech bro platform bosses and AI music innovators aren't getting inside.

In this book, we will follow the intrepid journey of the album all the way to the fort: its beginnings, its torrid existence through years of technological advancement and its refusal to capitulate in the age of digital music. We will even look to its future. I will draw on my own experience of working in the music business on many sides of the equation — at trade associations, labels, at Spotify, as a consultant to a variety of music business incumbents and innovators, and finally, as a writer, podcaster and music fan. For a few years, I switched off albums and immersed myself in playlists. I even launched a website of playlists across many different themes, genres and artists. It was a thoroughly enjoyable experience, and I loved playing the role of curator. But I really missed the album. When, after a few years, I returned to album listening, my brain took some time to adjust. Playlisting had fragmented my attention span across a wide variety of songs by different artists; compressed collections of songs that spanned twenty, thirty or forty years, squashing them together in a convenient time capsule. I found listening to whole albums again took some discipline: to retrain my brain, and for my ears to tune back in with a degree of patience I seemed to have lost — to embrace delayed gratification and accept a gradual familiarity and depth that can only come from repeated listens to a whole album.

It is albums that act as the gateway to a relationship between the artist and the fan. I feel like I know Queen, Thin Lizzy, The Police, a-ha, Björk, Duran Duran, Radiohead — my all-time favourites — because I have followed their journey album by album, knowing each record like the back of my own hand. Radiohead's albums have accompanied me through my entire adulthood. With each one, I lived a period of my life which became, in some way, intertwined and nourished by those records. *The Bends* accompanied me through an unsettled, rebellious early twenties. *OK Computer* had me joining an entire generation of Radiohead fans with a sense of belonging but also protest, while *Kid A* found me in a new phase as a responsible adult, married and a first-time parent. More recently, *A Moon Shaped Pool* reached me at a contented, steady stage of mid-life, fumbling through the ups and downs of a career, grown-up kids and old friendships; appreciating the album's complex personal, political, and spiritual themes, and its emotional, sonically delicate songs. Thom Yorke has talked about music as "fuel" — psychological nourishment — and that describes the impact of these albums on my life just perfectly. It is always a thrill to hear about a new Radiohead record — even if it must take ten years — I'm ready to receive the next one!

For listeners, albums can do this in a way that songs cannot — revealing our favourite artists to us in life stages. But we can only continue to enjoy this deeper type of fan relationship if we continue to embrace the album as something to consume in the foreground as well as the background. The vinyl resurgence helped a lot — dividing albums into two sides; nice chunks of time that aided my rehabilitation. Now, I'm right back into the world of albums. I don't bother to listen to singles, even new singles by favourite bands and artists. I'm happy to wait and hear them in the context of the album. I'm back into reading album reviews and devouring end-of-year best-of lists. I see and hear new artists only as album artists — if they can pass the ultimate test — to make enough good songs and put them in the right order to take me on a journey. Good songs are good songs. Playlists are a bunch of good songs. But albums are something much more than the sum of their parts. One of the best expressions I could find is by Edward Macan:

> Effectively tying together twenty of thirty minutes of music on both a musical and conceptual basis is a genuine compositional achievement, and a well-constructed multi-movement suite is able to impart a sense of monumentality and grandeur, to convey the sweep of experience, in a manner that a three or four minute song simply cannot.[1]

There are far too many records, of course, and never enough time. But if that's not one of those "first-world problems", then I don't know what is. Ultimately, an album is a conscious choice about how I want to spend my precious listening time. I'm certainly not going to give that over to the recommendation of an algorithm that has no concept of either art or time.

I'm never going back.

---

1 As quoted in Dai Griffiths's *33⅓* series on Radiohead's *OK Computer*.

Introduction

Going back to go forward, for the love of vinyl

When I turned fifty, I acquired a turntable and amplifier — a simple, analogue set-up. It was a gift to myself, on a modest budget, but a good excuse to salvage a pair of aging B&W 600 series bookend speakers from the loft. The only indulgent part of the package was the speaker cable and connectors. A hi-fi expert once told me that a modest set-up will do just fine, but do not skimp on the cabling. It's not an exaggeration to say that this decision transformed my life. Well, okay, perhaps that is a bit of a stretch, but in so many small ways, it's absolutely true. True enough for me to implore anyone and everyone who really calls themselves a music fan — therefore everyone — to do the same thing and switch to vinyl (allowing for the obvious constraints of space and disposable income). I already had an obsession with music, but that turntable (since put through one upgrade cycle, along with the amp and speakers) has seen a lot of action. It's been put to use, worked, utilised. It's been a very good investment.

From the first moment I set it up, there were so many pleasures to be had. I remember how my daughter, a digital native Gen Zer and phone addict, was blown away by the technology of the turntable. In a world where you can access just about anything with a few taps on a tiny screen, she was incredulous that by dropping a needle onto a record, it would then play this *enormous* sound — music in a way she had literally never heard before. Not through headphones, tiny computer speakers, a Bluetooth ghetto blaster or even in a live setting — but recorded music played back so that it fills the room. I'm not a technically minded person, so I couldn't explain how it worked. Of course, the miracles of modern technology meant that we could tap the phone and Google it at any time, but neither of us ever bothered. I don't think we really want to know. Why spoil the miracle?

My daughter has since inherited that first set-up from me and now has a modest vinyl collection, including the entire back catalogue of Radiohead albums (with the exception of *Pablo Honey*, obviously). She hunted down a copy of Kate Bush's *Hounds Of Love*, and, at one point, we arranged a listening session. We lay sprawled on the floor (well, I did; she chose the sofa and was allowed the privilege of looking at the record cover — no phones, mind!). This one forty minutes together is something we still talk about — quite a lot. Somehow, we've never got round to repeating the exercise, even though we often share lists of the next albums we will get to in our next, long awaited listening session. *Kid A* remains top of that list. I do cherish our *Hounds Of Love* session. It reminds me of long hours spent playing Canasta with my dad, or watching films late into the night together. Time spent in simple, immersive cultural activities — something that seems rarer between parents and their older kids these days.

The on-costs of acquiring a turntable can become significant, of course. I've bought around two hundred albums now, and each one has been played to the point of at least a few pops and crackles. And it's a joy. Music has never sounded so good. Music listening has actually become a proper "hobby" again, for the first time since my teenage years. It sounds simple, but this is a key part of the transformation I'm talking about. My house has a Bluetooth speaker in every room (I could never quite go with the piped multi-room system "solution"), but I would never have considered a night in playing music through a Bluetooth speaker. Now, though, every reasonable chance I get, if the family is out and my work is done for the day, there is an opportunity for a listening session. And it's a fantastic way to spend forty-five minutes — an effective antidote to the disorientating daze of browsing on a phone or vegging out to a box set on Netflix (or wasting forty-five minutes trying to find something to watch on Netflix!). These activities have become second-rate entertainment options compared with the ritual of playing records — dropping the needle, turning up the volume and kicking back on the sofa to just *listen*.

The lazy assessment would be to compare the cost of this investment with the availability of the very same records for virtually nothing, bundled in with an increasingly varied and dizzying choice of "content" on Spotify, but such comparisons are beside the point. I would have hardly listened to any of my vinyl albums on Spotify, and would almost certainly have had a different relationship with most of them.

Up to now, I have been of two minds on the vinyl resurgence. On the one hand, in the digitised twenty-first century, music as a physical product makes no sense. Why use up valuable scarce resources like paper, plastic, haulage and storage to deliver music that can now be packaged into a tiny digital file? Yet, it makes even less sense to think of music in bits and bytes. To load up a streaming app is not quite the "mini-fridge with no fucking beers in it", as Paul Weller described the first Apple iPod. Instead, streaming is more like having an industrial catering-sized fridge in your home, in which the abundant food is going out of date before you can eat it. The digitised forms of vinyl's contextual qualities — when turned into streaming platform features such as thumbnail covers, scrolling lyrics and often outdated artist biographies —seem soulless by comparison.

Author Will Self has the same problem with the digitised "printed" word. He said that reading a book on a Kindle or tablet "turned his brain to mush", and he could not enjoy the concept of "terrifying abundance". Most readers seem to agree. Look at where books are — real physical books — as a format, versus "e-books". The publishing industry is driven by the economic juggernaut that is physical books. While publishers have other formats, particularly audiobooks, they still invest the bulk of their efforts into marketing actual books. It will be fascinating to see whether Spotify's push into audiobooks will change that, but I doubt it. The vinyl record is not in the same mighty position as the physical book, having been supplanted in the mainstream consumption of music by other formats some five decades ago — yet it is a precious, growing format in music today.

Without a doubt, vinyl has transformed my music listening in recent years. I mostly fall short of the romantic ideal of putting a record on and doing nothing else but listening and staring at the cover and lyrics. That remains a fantasy, a memory of hundreds of hours doing just that as a teenager with the vast expanse of limitless time ahead. Yet, the very ritual of selecting the album off the shelf, taking the record out of the sleeve, sticking it on the turntable and finally dropping the tonearm onto the open grooves seems to encourage a more attentive form of listening — even if it is in the background while chopping vegetables or writing emails. It is a more elegant form of background music in a way that recalls the quote from Jean-Michel Basquiat: *"Art is how we decorate space; music is how we decorate time."* A music album can be background music, without being somehow reduced to the aural equivalent of wallpaper. After twenty minutes or so, you are brought back to the record's attention, should you want to hear more, and the connection between you and your choice of music is resumed.

Ultimately, one of the hidden pleasures of vinyl is that personal choice wins out over the terrifying abundance of streaming. The self-imposed scarcity of choosing a record and committing to a whole album (or at least one side) is liberating. You have done the discovery part and made a conscious choice. Now it's time to *enjoy* what you have chosen. With streaming, discovery and consumption often seem blurred together. Perhaps this was what Will Self was referring to with the digital word and his assessment of e-books as "brain mush": it is all too much information, everything available at once — an anxiety-inducing trade-off of precious time and endless "content".

If you are a music fan and have the means — and the time — it seems that more and more new music choices deserve to be vinyl purchases. After all, didn't the creators involved in making that music pour blood, sweat and tears into the craft? The least you can do as a fan is respect that by spending your hard-earned money on the music at a fair price. And then spending some quality time with it.

I am aware of a certain irony in succumbing to the vinyl revival. For decades, throughout the height of the CD boom during the 1980s and 1990s, the music industry didn't shy away from monetising "format chasers" — profiting massively, in no small part, from music fans repurchasing albums on CD that they had already owned before on vinyl (and, in some cases, twice: on vinyl and then cassette). Even applying a strict criteria to my vinyl purchases today, I find my most desirable list of albums I really want are those I previously owned — either on CD or, before that, on vinyl the first time around. The majority of music fans with vinyl collections from the initial LP era subsequently let their collections go (to the second-hand shops, charity shops and landfill sites) as they migrated to CD — marketed as a vastly superior technology and very clearly positioned as the endgame — an indestructible format that you would never ever need to replace. And now look where we are. Low and behold, the CD down went the very same treacherous path to obsolescence once followed by vinyl.

You might think things are different now. That music streaming really is the endgame. It's not. Streaming is only the latest "replacement cycle", the latest format chapter, in the lucrative history of recorded music. It's probably the most convenient, and certainly by far the most profitable, up to now. Just think, as you pony up your (steadily increasing) subscription fee, each and every single month, you are paying for the privilege of access to music you *might* like. Every time you play a song, it is costing you. If you stream an old song — maybe one from a CD or vinyl you once owned (or still might, if you check your loft, shed or garage) — it is costing you more than if you fished out the record and put it on. It may be in fractions too small to worry about, but it doesn't change the reality. The music industry is making money from every last drop of every stream — fractions that add up to billions of dollars for them. A streaming subscription may be amazing perceived value, but you are still paying for the stuff you already bought — except now you don't even own a copy. Should Spotify collapse tomorrow (and believe me, it might), you will be left raiding your loft or dashing out to the second-hand shops — or worse, subscribing to Deezer. Alas, a niche of music buyers seems to be starting again from the beginning — even if that means buying vinyl copies of recordings we previously owned, perhaps also on vinyl. Are we being dumb format chasers? Or are we forward-thinking, progressive fans looking to preserve the next generation of people who make the stuff we really do like listening to? What goes around comes around.

I could stop there, but there is more to say on the subject of how we listen to one of the greatest art forms available to us. So much, in fact, that I wrote this book about it. The album has been with us for seventy-five years, and, despite an onslaught of new technology and music formats over the decades, it has kept on going strong, mostly. I'll explore how this has happened and why it's such a good thing in these forthcoming chapters.

Ultimately, the album is aspirational for artists. It's the format that allows them to contribute to the canon of great recorded music works. To make your first album is a rite of passage. To make four, five or more albums is to build a catalogue and have the chance to leave a musical legacy. For fans, albums are also aspirational. A vinyl collection is a dignified way to recognise and enjoy the art form of popular music. A listening session is a journey we can share with the artist and with fellow listeners. And our classic album favourites are defining cultural episodes in our lives and become part of our own identity.

For these reasons, the format has refused to go away, despite technology trends, changes in music consumption and — as we'll see — some music industry decisions that didn't always give the album the best chance of survival. And, on the part of some tech companies, deliberate attempts to kill it stone dead. It's never going to happen — any more than Netflix killed movies. It's time to embrace the album, work with it, celebrate it and treasure it.

Let's start here.

Chapter 1
Spotify kills the album, almost

In 2016, I worked at Spotify, the Swedish tech firm and music streaming market leader. Having taken on board the suggestion from my boss to "help build bridges between the Product and Content orgs (tech short form for organisations)", I took myself off to Stockholm to join a meeting billed simply as "future formats discussion". At the meeting, I sat down in the offices of one of Spotify's technology Vice Presidents and a few others to brainstorm what Spotify might come up with next. The streaming service had already become dominant through its branded curated playlists (Rap Caviar, Hot Country, et al.), algorithmic playlists (Discover Weekly, Your Daily Mix) and launched a slew of innovative features such as Canvas — the short, looping visual wallpaper that accompanies almost every track you stream. But the desire was to do something bigger, more fundamental and, of course, more "disruptive" — the obligatory mission of all tech companies and corporate innovators around that time. The meeting was painful. It began with the VP giving a (not so) short lecture on the history of music formats, from the piano roll to streaming, and the transformed nature of music listening under Spotify's radical new "engagement model". The central problem was that none of these innovations had truly disrupted music formats — i.e., albums and songs — at least not yet. A song was still a song, and — more remarkably — an album was still an album. The implicated objective of the meeting (many of the objectives of tech firms are not explicitly spelled out but rather worded euphemistically) was to change this. Why on earth, in the unstoppable ascendancy of streaming, would "users" bother to engage with *albums*? After all, the album was a music industry construct, a manufactured format that had endured only because the industry persisted in ramming it down consumers' throats. A pretty exciting premise for a business meeting, then.

So much was true. The music industry had become structured around the album in almost every way — artist contracts, product creation, packaging and distribution, pricing and profit. Prevailing wisdom was that, historically, roughly one in ten albums went into the black, but some of those would become so successful as to more than offset the losses of the other nine. Music was always a risky business and a tricky business model to wrap your head around. This business model, however, was being dismantled in front of our eyes — the irreversible shift from music ownership to access, via a monthly subscription to music's entire library of two hundred million songs. It would only be a matter of time (a year or two?) before the anachronism of the album was no more. Obliterated. Banished to the annals of corporate and cultural history.

Fortunately, that did not happen. I can imagine this meeting was one of a thousand such discussions at Spotify and elsewhere during the hypergrowth period of streaming. Meanwhile, over at record labels and among the artist community, a different flavour of discussion on the same topic was also frequently had — well, perhaps not so much discussion as a continuous rumble of questions. Why do our artists still want to make albums? What happens when the album is finally dead? How can the music business survive on just… songs!? All reasonable, logical questions. Trouble was, nobody had any good answers.

Back to that meeting. After a prolonged introduction, as the discussion progressed, I felt obliged to share some important points to fill in gaps in the VP's oral history of the music business — namely, the curious case of the album's origins:

> Early in the twentieth century,[2] the term "album" was first used to describe collections that record owners of 78s used to put together in a book-like format, similar to a photo album. These albums were used to compile classical music works, operas and collections of popular songs. Thus, not really an industry construct so much as an industry response to consumer demand.

Naturally this put the discussion on a different footing, momentarily, before someone in the meeting asked a clarifying question: "What do you mean, '78s'?"

Much has already been written about how streaming has changed music and the listening habits of millions. There's no need to dwell on that here, although a form of shorthand is to look no further than Spotify Wrapped, the annual statistical summary of your own personal listening habits on the platform. Wrapped deals in time (minutes and months), songs, genres, artists and podcasts. In doing so, you may have noticed that albums are not included. That reflects listener behaviours

---

2 In 1909, according to *The History of Music Production*, by Richard James Burgess (OUP), p. 19.

on the platform but is also instructive as to Spotify's views on the format. Culturally, it's surprisingly out of touch with the way many music fans and artists still think about music.

Let's face it, Spotify and the other tech platforms that have grown music's consumption over the past two decades have not exactly been friendly to the industry's flagship format. This was well illustrated by a run-in between Spotify and Adele — one of the world's biggest recording artists — in 2021. Adele requested (very politely, it must be said) that Spotify remove the default shuffle option for albums. Previously, Spotify's big green "Play" button on album pages automatically shuffled tracks when users hit play on an album. Adele argued that albums are carefully crafted by artists to tell a story or convey a particular journey, and the default shuffle disrupted that intention. She tweeted about the change, saying:

> This was the only request I had in our ever-changing industry! We don't create albums with so much care and thought into our track listing for no reason. Our art tells a story and our stories should be listened to as we intended. Thank you Spotify for listening.

Spotify capitulated, quickly changing the default setting for albums to play tracks in order, allowing listeners to experience albums as artists intended. The decision was widely praised by artists and fans, highlighting the importance of respecting creative intent in the music industry. The whole episode blew over pretty quickly after that. But let's stop and think about this for a moment. Spotify had, arbitrarily, set automatic shuffle… on *all* albums — on ***Dark Side Of The Moon***, on ***Thriller***, on ***OK Computer*** (what if it started with "Fitter Happier"!?) and on *Abbey Road* (when did the medley come in, I wonder!?). A move like that has bluster, but it barely disguises indifference towards a format so critical to its largest trade partners — one that is central to the culture of music as an art form and makes up a substantial part of the history of recorded music. Spotify introduced the album shuffle option as the default playback mode sometime after the launch of the platform in 2008, but the exact date is unclear. It's somewhat remarkable that more information isn't available on the subject — or that there wasn't more of an industry outcry at the time (let alone music label bosses actually allowing it to happen at all). The Adele incident is all the more remarkable because it took an intervention by an artist — one of the world's most successful — to get the feature corrected. It was perhaps a sign of the times as to where the album was positioned in 2021. The prevailing mood in the music business was that the album's days were numbered, so perhaps it wasn't such a big deal to try to stop Spotify accelerating the inevitable. However, arguably, Adele's intervention was a significant victory and a turning point for the format, along with the increasing momentum in vinyl sales, which began to reach a peak shortly afterwards. Clearly, default album shuffle mode was a deliberate move by Spotify — likely as part of the company's drive to dominate music discovery through playlist-based listening or, more broadly, to "control the demand for music". To tech leaders, the album represents the establishment, and the establishment was something to be taken down. If that meant the album format was collateral damage, so be it.

Of course, the album had already withstood serious threats way before Spotify's automatic shuffle mode. Between 1999 and 2008, Napster and iTunes teamed up to unbundle the album. First, Napster atomised the entire history of recorded music by making songs — every song — available for free. Steve Jobs's answer to this music industry cataclysm was then to offer individual songs for the breathtakingly reasonable price of 79 cents/pence via the iTunes download store.

For almost a decade before streaming and subscriptions began to take hold, the album was subjected to a bruising from the early days of what I refer to as music's "song economy" — a seismic shift towards single songs, turning the entire music business into one big "celestial jukebox". The threat from Napster was obvious, as was the music industry's response. But iTunes was a different beast altogether: an industry-backed, perfectly legal alternative to the way music had been packaged and sold for the previous five decades.

When Steve Jobs launched iTunes in 2004 and revealed the 79p price point, the press gang in the audience gave out a genuine collective gasp (I was sitting among them and still remember exactly how it *sounded* – probably something similar, I would imagine, to the cinema audience watching the final scene of *Planet of the Apes* in 1968). This new product would allow music buyers to cherry-pick their favourite songs and, in doing so, avoid having to buy the album altogether. But it would do so at a price point bang on the equivalent of the average price of a song on a CD album (roughly £10.40/13). There was no premium required for cherry-picking privileges whatsoever, just a healthy discount on what had been the previous price of a CD single. It really was breathtaking.

Thus, the music industry — whether bravely or stupidly — fully encouraged music fans to gut the album format that had become the industry's foundation. In the face of this brutal assault, however, the album somehow remained intact. This is more remarkable for the fact that the prior two decades — the CD era — had bloated albums to extra length, higher prices and lower value, essentially driving the format into the ground as a rip-off product. The expectation was that 79p songs (or the free alternative) would kill off the album in no time.

Compared to all this, streaming's multi-pronged attack on the album was, arguably, less brutal but more insidious. If Napster and iTunes unbundled the album, Spotify merely did its best to ignore it. Streaming has not been kind to the album, but it hasn't killed it either. Indeed, it's possible — though hard to prove — that artists and record makers have raised their game when it comes to albums. They've got better — shorter, leaner, more thematic. So, perhaps it's time that music distribution platforms recognised that they can't always get what they want. Sometimes it just isn't possible to disrupt culture that's bigger and more enduring than any phase or chapter of technology. I'm talking about the fact that art can sometimes buck the market.

Spotify has indeed come around. In March 2023, the streaming service introduced its Countdown Pages feature, enabling fans to pre-save upcoming albums, preview track lists, watch exclusive video clips, purchase merchandise and view a countdown timer leading up to the release. Initially available to select artists, Spotify expanded the feature to all eligible artists with at least five thousand active listeners in July 2024. More was to come. In May 2025 Spotify launched the Countdown Charts, which rank the most pre-saved (i.e. pre-released) albums across the platform. This is Spotify's take on an album chart, listing a global Top 10 records anyone has yet to hear in full.

In 2024, Spotify introduced Spotify CLASSICS, described as "our first-ever program to celebrate catalog music". The launch copy was conciliatory on the album format:

> Streaming has transformed not only the way fans listen to music, but also the way artists release music to the world. And while music has become a more song-driven culture in recent years, that doesn't mean albums have lost their impact. With the introduction of Spotify Classics: Hip-Hop & RNB Albums of the Streaming Era, we're celebrating the classic albums that have stood the test of time, no matter the era.

At last, it seemed that Spotify began to see the album as something for the streaming era to *celebrate* after all. That said, the series abruptly halted after just one edition, likely cut as an editorial luxury that was surplus to requirements as the platform shifted its focus relentlessly to the algorithm.

You would think that Spotify's hesitation on albums would be an invitation for its competitors to step in, but that hasn't happened. The best the collective competition has come up with so far is Apple Music's 2024 initiative to define the "100 Best Albums" (of all time), a ten-day countdown Apple kicked off in May 2024. The trouble with this particular list was that nobody needed it. Besides, there was a lack of transparency as to the criteria used to derive the list, other than the vague statement about it being "assembled with artists and experts". Those artists clearly did not include any of Johnny Cash, Dolly Parton, Diana Ross or the Who — or indeed any country music artists except Kacey Musgraves (her album *Golden Hour* was the only country title included, despite country music's heavy ascendancy in the last five years or so). *The Guardian*'s culture editor, Gwilym Mumford, wrote a sarcastic review:

> Noticing an absence of best-of lists from media publications, record stores and the like these days, those disruptors at Apple Music have taken it upon themselves to compile a list of their 100 best albums of all time.

Nobody could accept the list as having any credibility, and the initiative backfired, with Apple Music subjected to a ribbing across social media. In collaboration with luxury publisher Assouline, Apple Music released a limited-edition coffee table book. Available to the record buying public for $450, the book sported a white linen hardcover with gold gilding on the page edges and spine lettering, housed in a translucent acrylic slipcase etched with the Apple Music logo. Now the album is a format to be celebrated, yes, but that does seem a little elitist. It's unlikely anyone in a pub quiz will know the answer to what was chosen as No. 1, not that any pub quizmaster is about to ask.

Never mind. At least Apple Music did *something*. The point, perhaps, is that the album is once again accepted — one way or another — by its two largest previous assassins. Of the current crop of music streaming platforms, the niche French service Qobuz seems to treat the album with the most respect, placing new album releases front and centre in the app's carousels and featuring a genuiney eclectic editorial mix, without a sniff of algorithmic nonesense. Now the game is on to find ways to celebrate, innovate and perhaps even improve the music industry's jewel in the crown: the humble "LP".

Chapter 2
An alternative/personal history of the album

The album's history is fairly well documented, so I don't mean to repeat it all here. Instead, I want to briefly acknowledge others' efforts in documenting the album's journey. The majority of stuff I've read about the album is very much in homage to the vinyl LP. By comparison, you'd be hard pushed to find a genuine CD enthusiast these days, although I'm sure there are a few. What interests me most is that almost every music fan of a certain age has their own personal album history. In the book *Long Players: Writers on the Albums that Shaped Them*,[3] *New Statesman* Editor Tom Gatti compiles superb accounts by writers of the albums they cherish, all of which express so well the deep connection we have with albums. In Gatti's introduction, he notes that when he first moved into a flat with his wife, the two of them kept their vinyl collections separate. Not an uncommon state of affairs, I would speculate, especially since everyone has their own particular way of arranging a record collection, be it alphabetical (first name, or surname?), by decade, genre, recency or colour of the album spine. We are nothing if not precious about our record collections and

---

3 *Long Players: Writers on the Albums that Shaped Them*, Tom Gatti (Bloomsbury).

deeply passionate about which albums we label our favourites. The history of the album is essentially a collective history of the billions of people who have played them, owned them and claimed emotional ownership over those they cherish as favourites. Perhaps this is really the reason why the format has proved so resilient in the onslaught of multiple assaults from technology. We have an innate need to preserve an art form that cuts deep.

In the art book *Why Vinyl Matters: A Manifesto from Musicians and Fans*,[4] Jennifer Otter Bickerdike takes a passionate deep dive into the folklore of vinyl through a series of great interviews with well-known and renowned artists, songwriters, music industry luminaries and other vinyl enthusiasts. Jen's foreword is no less expressive than any of them, as she recounts her own vinyl awakening through the Go-Go's 1984 album *Talk Show*:

> The full experience of that record, of sitting for hours singing along to the lyrics provided by the album sleeve, trying to capture the effortless punk chic of the band as they appeared on the cover — provided a guide for my emerging teenage character.

If you will indulge me, I'll tell you about my beginnings with albums, in which the undisputed star is the once deeply unfashionable and now resurgent rock band Queen. I'll be quick, but it is important to the album's story — as well as to my own album story. Before I do that, I want to mention three other critical album books that deserve some serious credit.

---

4 *Why Vinyl Matters: A Manifesto from Musicians and Fans*, Jennifer Otter Bickerdike (ACC Editions).

In *A Fabulous Creation: How the LP Saved Our Lives*,[5] David Hepworth's imperious volume on the album's imperious period (1967–1982), the music scholar and journalist dives deep into the well of nostalgia, concluding that: "I don't believe in records changing lives. What I do believe is that records we liked can lead us back to the lives we once led and the people we once were."

Travis Elborough's *The Long-Player Goodbye* is another nostalgia trip, diving deep into the album's origins and its many interpretations by classic artists and iconic labels. Elborough's love letter to the format is a detailed delight, charting its evolution from 78s to LPs, cassettes, CDs and then digital downloads and streaming. The book was written in 2008 and more or less assumes the album is on its way out — not an unreasonable assumption, as we'll see. That in itself makes the book more interesting to revisit now.

Lastly, not just one book about albums but a whole series. If you have yet to hear about or try the 33⅓ series of books, you should start now. Widely acclaimed by fans, musicians and scholars alike, the series started out in rambling fashion (series creator David Barker originally commissioned the first few volumes, neglecting to provide the authors any guidelines, so each book can come at the album from a completely different angle) but has become an established and thriving brand — something that very much reflects the power of the album format and celebrates it in the best possible way. Just pick your favourite record among those covered and get going. As Barker wrote about them:

---

5 *A Fabulous Creation: How the LP Saved Our Lives*, David Hepworth (Penguin Random House).

> This series is based on the idea that when we fall in love, we want to immerse ourselves in the object of our love. We want to know the history, the backstory - and often, we want to know what other people think. Surely we can't be the only ones to feel this way about "Veronica Mars," about Jonathan Coe…or about Led Zeppelin IV?

And so, to my own little piece of album history. For many album fans, parents play a significant role, and I'm no exception — although the house I grew up in really had one of the sorriest vinyl album collections to ever exist. It consisted of no more than ten titles, of which I remember Gilbert O'Sullivan's *I'm a Writer, Not a Fighter* (1973), with its distinctive green cover, a John Denver album, and a Barbara Dickson album, but neither of them was an original release nor official greatest hits — both run off as part of some obscure budget line of compilation records that existed in the 1970s. More credible entries were Johnny Cash's *At San Quentin* and two titles by The Beatles: *A Hard Day's Night* and *Rubber Soul*. The others I just cannot remember, but that's because they were forgettable. It was an anti-collection and we had nothing to play them on anyhow, our "music centre" was very much a cassette-centric set-up. Our collection of cassettes was larger, more current, but equally random. We had ELO, Smokey, Status Quo, Roy Orbison, ABBA and a few chart hit compilations.

I still recall spending time sifting through those albums, though. The object holds wonder and mystery, even if you cannot actually play them. Perhaps that explains why young music fans now have vinyl LP collections but no turntable, the playing of the actual records merely a future possibility, an aspiration.

At some stage, though, I acquired a turntable — one of the cheap ones with the automatic tonearm. You flicked the switch and watched the Heath Robinson chain of events unfold until the needle clunked down on the groove. For the most part, I acquired singles: Madness, XTC, The Police, UB40. Among these were my all-time favourite singles — "Don't Stop Me Now", "Crazy Little Thing Called Love", "Play The Game" and "Flash" — all, of course, by Queen. These four songs became the stepping stones to my first-ever album — one of the most significant albums I have ever acquired: Queen's *Greatest Hits*. Released in 1981, the first volume of Queen's singles was the first experience I had of the concept of the truly ubiquitous record. Simply everyone had to have a copy, whether they saved their own pocket money, relied on their parents to want it enough to buy a household copy or, as I did, make it top of their Christmas list. Queen's *Greatest Hits* is pure album gold. The cover is glorious, the inner sleeve notes pithy write-ups of each of the songs — some of the best label copy I've ever read. The genius, though, was to link the little write-up of each of the songs on the record back to its original album, with a little thumbnail picture of the album cover. I read those inner sleeve notes over and over. I knew I had to get my hands on each of those albums. If these songs had sprung from those wells, then what other delights did each one contain?

Having secured a weekend job picking potatoes or planting onions, after two day's back-breaking work I would collect the princely pay packet of £5. But £5 was enough. The whole catalogue of Queen albums was stocked (precisely one copy each, mind) in the music department, top floor of the House Of Fraser department store in Paragon Square, Hull, and my plan was to pick them off one by one. They were not cheap, priced between £5 and £6, but that meant I could buy one each weekend I picked up my wages — just about. I had scouted the territory multiple times before I could buy my first one, worried that if someone else bought one of the copies, then that would be it — chance gone. Over the course of the summer of 1982, I got the job done. I can even remember the order I bought the albums in (the first was *News Of The World*, the last *Queen II*) — not chronologically but simply by instinct, or on impulse right there in the shop — it was pure *desire*.

At the time of writing this book, Queen's *Greatest Hits* has sold over twenty-five million copies worldwide, solidifying its status as one of the best-selling albums of all time. In the UK alone, it holds the distinction of being the best-selling album ever, with sales over seven million (a milestone reached in July 2022, some forty years after its release, making it the first album in UK chart history to achieve such a feat). In the United States, the album has been certified nine times Platinum, indicating over nine million sales. It reached the Top 10 of the Billboard 200 chart for the first time in November 2020, four decades after I unwrapped it on Christmas morning.

Queen slow-burned their way to becoming one of the biggest pop bands in the world, navigating all of music's major format eras: LP, cassette, CD, downloads and eventually streaming. There was a long period (most of the 1990s and a fair chunk of the 2000s) when nobody really cared much for Queen's music. It took a steady succession of rereleases and related cultural events to change this. The first major initiative was by Universal Music Group, which released remastered versions of all of Queen's albums in the "super-deluxe" CD jewel case.[6] This was part of a broader fortieth-anniversary celebration of Queen, following a transfer of the band's recorded music rights from EMI to Universal Music in late 2010. The albums were released in batches throughout 2011, with each featuring improved remastering and some editions including "deep cuts" — bonus tracks.

It was the beginning of a reboot for the band that just kept on going: massive legacy tours (with Adam Lambert a more successful stand-in for Freddie than Paul Rodgers had been), documentaries, the blockbuster *Bohemian Rhapsody* movie, major sync deals and social media phenomena (do not underestimate the power of those Freddie memes) steadily elevated Queen from outside the top two hundred and into the top fifty most consistently streamed bands in the world. By the time I wrote this, Queen were notching up fifty million monthly listeners on Spotify.

In today's song-driven music economy, Queen is an "uncorrelated" earnings monster. All of the above-mentioned phenomena have helped weave Queen's music into the fabric of Western culture across generations. For Gen Z and millennials, it's the hit songs that remain irresistible (remember those "Bohemian Rhapsody" reaction videos on YouTube?). Boomers continue to absorb Queen's top songs without a drop of boredom. How could we ever get bored of songs like "Don't Stop Me Now" or "Somebody To Love"?

But where does Queen's album catalogue fit into this equation as we speak? Queen's big breakthrough moment

---

6 In fact, the Super Jewel Case wasn't great. The 2008 EMI reissues of the Queen albums, in collaboration with the Spanish Newspaper *El Mundo*, were much more aesthetically pleasing. Those are rarities on Discogs now.

was 1975, with "Bohemian Rhapsody" and the album it came from, *A Night at the Opera*, both phenomenal successes that became major contributions to rock legend. From that moment on, Queen straddled the twin successes of being both a big singles band but at the same time a band whose career is clearly written in album-shaped chapters. But how many fans under the age of forty — streaming or engaging with "Bo Rhap" in some way — have ever even listened to *A Night at the Opera* or even know that the song and album are joined at the hip?

It's an intriguing question, given the sheer size of Queen as a modern music industry commodity. Queen's catalogue is now the biggest rights acquisition deal in music business history. In 2024, Sony Music spent £1 billion to acquire a substantial proportion of Queen Productions copyrights. What upsides might lie ahead to reignite the band's catalogue further, and what role, if any, will their albums play in continuing to mine their cultural capital?

It's possible that this process has indeed begun. Over half a century since its release, Queen's self-titled 1973 debut was rereleased in 2024 (just in time for Christmas), as a box set package, including a new track listing, alternative takes, demos and live tracks and other "rather lovely purple things", as drummer Roger Taylor expressed it — referring to a 108-page book containing handwritten lyrics and memorabilia. The album was remixed and restored "to sound the way the band always wanted it to" and was hailed as the very first time that a Queen album has ever received a new stereo mix. Brian May himself was keen to promote the record as "not just a remaster" but "a brand-new 2024 rebuild of the entire Queen debut album, which, with the benefit of hindsight, we have re-titled *Queen I*. *Queen I* is the debut album we always dreamed of bringing to you."

Like other Queen fans of a certain age, I lapped it up (I didn't buy the box set but the new stereo mix proved the perfect excuse to revisit an album I would never otherwise have gone back to). The potential of the rest of the Queen album catalogue isn't so straightforward, yet somehow I feel like the record industry — Sony Music, in this case — will pull off another magic trick. It will conjure up a way to make Queen's albums desirable, collectible, essential. The available tools of stereo remixes, remasters and rare and unreleased archive recordings have now received a major addition to their arsenal: augmentative and generative artificial intelligence. Just imagine what could be done with Freddie's voice enhancements to previously unreleased material (as hinted with the 2022 single "Face It Alone"). When it comes to reinventing the wheel, the recording industry is not to be underestimated. This is demonstrated by the following potted history of the album's previously marketed formats.

Format chasers — the music industry's cash cow

Was I correct to tell Spotify that the album was invented by the fan? It seems only a partial truth in the end. The first manufactured long-playing record is attributed to Columbia Records, proof there was a time when record labels could also innovate new products. When Columbia ran press ads for its latest invention, it did so with the strapline: "45 minutes of music from a single record… another 'first' by Columbia Records." How often can a record label of the twenty-first century make a claim like that! Introduced in 1948 and launched at a press conference in New York, the 12-inch vinyl record spun at 33⅓ rpm and could hold up to twenty-two minutes of music per side. This allowed artists to compile multiple songs into a single disc, and therefore record buyers to purchase those songs in one convenient package. It's unlikely that this replaced a mass habit of collecting single discs together in photo books, but the LP was almost certainly designed to appeal initially to classical music fans who could now obtain longer whole classical pieces on one disc.

Of course, this being the music industry, it took all of nine months before a rival record company launched a rival format. The 45 rpm single was launched by RCA and designed to compete directly with Columbia Records' invention. This launched a history of format wars in the music business, often between rival label camps, as we'll see later. Of course, the single and the album settled into a co-existence and later became symbiotic as music fans often bought and collected both. And fifty years after Columbia Records launched the album, RCA and Columbia also came together as a team, when Sony Music (which had bought Columbia in 1988) acquired RCA's parent company, Bertelsmann Music Group (BMG). Such circularity is very much part of the music industry's nature.

Early albums were classical works, soundtracks, musicals and niche folk and jazz. A curious early best-selling genre on the LP was spoken-word comedy. By the 1950s, comedians began using the LP to release full-length stand-up performances, sketches and monologues. In 1960, at the third Annual GRAMMY awards, comedian Bob Newhart's *The Button-Down Mind of Bob Newhart* won Album of the Year while the future sitcom star took Best New Artist.

When it comes to claiming the title of first ever pop album, history seems to converge on a small bunch of contenders. Frank Sinatra's *Songs for Young Lovers* (1954) was one of the first albums designed as a cohesive listening experience. The run of albums that followed — in which Sinatra was put together with arranger Nelson Riddle, nicknamed "The Capitol Years" — were the forerunners of what later became known as the concept album, one of the format's true super powers. It took a few more years before writer-performer artists made albums made of entirely original compositions — with *Buddy Holly*, his 1958 debut, considered one of the first and, in some ways, the dawn of the rock & roll album as we know it. But no album milestone can exclude The Beatles, whose third album, *A Hard Day's Night* (1964), was the first in which a band wrote and recorded every song themselves: all thirteen tracks being written by John Lennon and Paul McCartney. Of course, *A Hard Day's Night* makes a nicely convenient example of the album's ultimate longevity. If that record was truly the birth of the pop music album format, then its sixtieth anniversary perhaps deserved a bigger celebration than it received. Instead, we can expect a greater jamboree in 2027 — the sixtieth anniversary of *Sgt. Pepper's Lonely Hearts Club Band*, The Beatles' 1967 classic and the first all-encompassing execution of the concept album.[7]

It is indeed the Fab Four to whom we must attribute the album's coming of age. The Beatles are the first band whose career is mapped by way of their album catalogue — a famously prolific run of thirteen official studio albums across just seven years between 1963 and 1970. After the Beatles,

[7] Others got to the concept album before The Beatles. Frank Sinatra's *In the Wee Small Hours* (1955) and The Beach Boys' *Pet Sounds* (1966) are clear examples. However, *Sgt. Pepper's* took the concept further by integrating its theme into every aspect of the album — music, lyrics, production and packaging — making it a landmark in the history of popular music.

we essentially landed on planet Album — where, in Jack Antonoff's words, there's "no brilliant artist that hasn't existed for a real period of time and changed things, and has a real audience that isn't based on albums". All the brilliant album artists began to arrive in their wake, during the 1970s — the glory decade of the vinyl LP: The Rolling Stones, Led Zeppelin, Fleetwood Mac, Pink Floyd, The Who and David Bowie; artists almost as relevant today as they were then.

Lastly, I might add some serious credit to Led Zeppelin for the band's debut album. Although by 1969 the rock & roll album had well and truly arrived, Jimmy Page was determined that the hottest new rock band in the world, newly signed to the hottest label in America (Atlantic Records), would launch exclusively as an album band. Page was adamant that singles were off the agenda: "I'd seen singles break bands and I didn't want that; I wanted us to be an album band."[8] Page had been inspired by the emergence in the US of "album-oriented rock" (AOR). FM radio stations such as San Francisco's KSAN and LA based KMET had adopted a trend for playing full album sides and deeper cuts than anything previously played by radio. Now if there was ever a trend that needed to come back around today, that's the one.

Jimmy Page famously stuck with the "album band" manifesto throughout Led Zeppelin's eight-album run, through to 1979 and up until the band's abrupt, tragic end (drummer John Bonham died in 1980). Even after he had penned a bona fide hit for the follow-up to Led Zeppelin, in the form of the rifftastic "Whole Lotta Love", Page took the single out of the song by way of inserting a one-minute, forty-five-second-long

---

8 Jimmy Page, interviewed for *Becoming Led Zeppelin*, Sony Pictures Classics, 2025.

experimental section (referred to by music writer Mark Blake as a "breathless orgasm") a mere eighty seconds into the track itself. You couldn't get away with it then, and you can't get away with it now, but it didn't stop Page. Alas, it didn't stop the song being a massive radio hit either, and it was the band's only single to go Gold in America. After their debut, Led Zeppelin ascended to become the world's biggest rock band throughout the 1970s, their album-band philosophy influencing countless others, Pink Floyd, Rush, Black Sabbath and indeed Queen.

Sticking to an alternative history, then, let's cut to the chase. The imperious days of the pop & rock album, as documented in David Hepworth's *A Fabulous Creation*, run in parallel with the vinyl LP: 1967 to 1982. There is no need to reinvent that wheel here. The most evocative writing I have found about that illustrious period comes courtesy of Aubrey Powell, one of the three founders of Hipgnosis, the legendary design agency behind the most iconic album cover sleeves of the 1970s. In his book *Vinyl. Album. Cover. Art: The Complete Hipgnosis Catalogue*, Powell sums up the format and the time thus:

> Vinyl occupied a large space in any home and often took pride of place on a sitting-room shelf next to gigantic amplifiers and speakers. Boasting about how many records you had in your collection became a major pastime and what kind of music you bought told others what kind of person you were. The covers gave an inkling of your personality, your musical tastes and preferences, and just how up to date and hip you were. Then there was the ritual of buying a new record, or perhaps choosing another, sometimes solely influenced by the nature of

> the cover design. Once home, you ripped off the shrink wrap, carefully keeping the outer stickers. You eased out the vinyl from the cardboard cover without making a scratch, placed it on your record deck, and dropped the needle onto the record itself. You sat back, enjoyed the sounds and studied the one connection between you and the band: the cover. Soaking up the lyrics, the information, the text, the credits, the band photos, the free stickers, postcard and poster and most importantly looking for clues in the front cover. What was the artist up to now?

Although Powell's words about the vinyl set-up at home and record collections describe the stereotype of the aficionado, the record buying and listening experience is perfectly captured. I must have spent hours, possibly days, staring at the central photograph of the inner gatefold cover of Queen's *Jazz* album as that record played. It captured the band in the recording studio (Mountain Studios in Montreux, Switzerland, which Queen purchased after making *Jazz*). John Deacon stands in one corner behind a rack of guitars; Roger Taylor is reclined into his drum seat with his feet up; while Brian May actually waves right at the camera — at *me* and the other owners of *Jazz*. Freddie is nowhere to be seen, which is just as curious a part of the photograph as anything in it. Except, look again and there he is, lying flat on his stomach on the grand piano, between Deacon and Taylor. Talk about "What was the artist up to now" — it was there for you to see.[9] I read the label copy on that inner sleeve

---

9 Infamously, *Jazz* also came with a free poster: a three-way foldout

over and over. Bicycles supplied by Halfords. Concept by Queen. Sleeve Design by Cream. Thunderbolt Courtesy of God! This album is dedicated to John Harris (who is/was John Harris?). And where was the usual "No synthesisers" disclaimer that had concluded the sleeve notes on previous Queen albums?

Of course, all this was soon to be a thing of the past, thanks to the fast-approaching advance of the music industry's first digital battering ram: the compact disc. By the time Queen released the *Jazz* album in all its gatefold glory, the technical specifications for the CD were being bounced between two corporation headquarters in the Netherlands and Japan. Combining Philips's expertise in optical disc technology with Sony's digital encoding systems, the resulting product (and its accompanying player, the Sony CDP-101) was to offer a "revolutionary new way to experience music, offering superior sound quality and durability compared to vinyl records and cassette tapes". The first music CD sold to the public was Billy Joel's *52nd Street*, released on 1 October 1982, in Japan. I wonder how that dubious accolade sits with the legend, who has never seemed impressed with record industry milestones. That year, total music industry revenues from record sales were $12 billion. By 1990, they would be worth double.

Between the last hurrah for the vinyl LP and the ubiquitous onslaught of the CD was squeezed not only the cassette but also a raft of gimmicks, including coloured vinyl, picture disc, bonus singles and other paraphernalia aimed at the avid record collector and the conspicuous show-offs described by Aubrey

---

landscape shot of the start of a bike race featuring sixty-five nude women. As a thirteen-year-old, I spent almost as long looking at that picture — though not quite.

Powell. It meant that music superfans would find themselves classed as format chasers, described by David Hepworth as being enthralled in "a long and needlessly costly marriage to just one record that had a habit of turning round every few years and demanding to be purchased again in a previously unsuspected form, and always at a higher price".

If the CD was to eventually attain a bad reputation, it was in large part because it ushered in the music industry's first-ever almost-compulsory "replacement cycle". Whether your record collection had leaned towards the purism of vinyl or the convenience of the cassette, the CD was now positioned to surpass and replace both those formats in every way. Music buyers were left with no real choice but to get on board with the new digital technology or face being "left behind". A similar message would echo as the digital music era kicked in early in the new century.

While music executives expected CDs to be successful, the speed and scale at which they replaced vinyl and cassettes took the music industry by surprise. But if record companies excel in any area of commerce, it's reacting quickly to dollar signs. Record labels were aware that some music fans would probably replace their existing music collections on CD, and they quickly embraced tactics to encourage it. They became masters at reselling, using the CD's digital capability and extra capacity to the full: remasters, bonus tracks, expanded liner notes or special packaging — all designed to entice fans to repurchase music they already owned. By the mid-1980s, CDs had become the dominant format, far surpassing vinyl and cassettes in sales. The CD had become worth its weight in gold, a license to print money. And yet nobody felt like it was easy to love. After the warmth of vinyl and/or cassette, the CD ushered in the colder, sterile atmosphere of digital music.

Throughout the 1990s, the good times rolled for the music business. Now virtually a monopoly format, CD prices were free to drift upwards, and nobody minded or even noticed much, since the 1990s boomed both economically and in music terms, literally — the biggest strength of the CD being its ubiquity: it could be played by almost anybody, almost anywhere. The Sony Discman was a slicker (if duller) version of the iconic Walkman. Flash in-car CD systems, some of which could load multiple discs at a time, were installed as standard. And by now every household had replaced their turntable or cassette stereos with CD-tray home music systems available at every conceivable price point upwards of $100. Music retail capitalised on this with more, ever larger megastores. It's quaint to think about it now, but the in-store merchandising of a CD title was as important to its sales and chart success as having a song playlisted on the radio. The footfall in music stores swept up ardent fans and casual buyers alike. Indeed, the overlap between these categories was named the "fifty-pound man" (this time it was a friend of David Hepworth's, but when Hepworth mentioned this particular breed of music fan to the UK music industry at a BPI annual gathering, it went down as music marketing legend, at least in Britain, as the "fifty-quid bloke"). The UK was still the world's third-largest music market, after the US and Japan, but with Britpop on the march, it punched well above its weight in terms of music talent exports. Record labels seemed to sign bands if they could all turn up to the studio and play something, anything. This was all down to the CD boom. As a music boss said to me when I first joined the IFPI in January 2000: "Technology has always been a friend to our industry." With Napster looming, this had been true until it wasn't.

Other than lining the pockets of music moguls, what did the CD really do for the album format? For one thing, the album got substantially longer, sometimes for better, but as time went on, it seemed mostly for worse. CDs could hold up to eighty minutes of music — almost twice as much as vinyl or cassette. This led to longer track lists, more experimentation, but also "filler" songs that would never have made it onto a tighter vinyl LP. The Smashing Pumpkins' *Mellon Collie and the Infinite Sadness* (1995) is one such example: a two-hour long double album issued as a double CD, hailed by some as a masterpiece but others as a dreary sprawl of a record that was all but impossible to get through in one piece let alone in one sitting. I quite like the album personally.

Of course, a major change was the dispensing with the album's two sides. Vinyl and cassettes required flipping over, creating intentional "Side A" and "Side B" structures. In some cases, this was central to the album's whole concept. Take the 1981 album *Penthouse & Pavement*, the debut of Sheffield band Heaven 17 (ranked the fifth-best album of 1981 by the NME). Pre-CD and conceived as a true concept album (about right-wing libertarian fascist capitalism!), with vinyl in mind, Side A of the record is electro-funk, inspired by Motown, James Brown and Chic, whereas Side B gives way to hard-core, stripped-down electronics. For anyone buying the record on CD format a year or two later, the concept was all but lost.

On the other hand, the CD made albums feel like one continuous experience. Some artists designed albums with a midpoint in mind. Radiohead's *OK Computer* has a natural breakpoint in the form of "Fitter Happier". This might form a large part of a theory of Suede's singer Brett Anderson, whose band broke through at the height of the CD era, that "track seven" on an album has to offer something interesting, or be good enough to make the listener's ears prick up and see things through to the end. Albums without interruptions, especially longer ones, could feel like more epic, unfolding journeys. I always felt this way listening to U2's *Achtung Baby*, which I hear move through three distinct phases of 4:4:3 in terms of song sequence (those closing three songs are still my all-time favourite trio of songs to close any album). Another example is Björk's *Vespertine*, this time in 4:3:4:1 song sequence.

Many classic albums from the CD period feel like the continuous journey is central to their impact. R.E.M.'s *Automatic for the People* (1992), Green Day's *Dookie* (1994), Suede's *Dog Man Star* (1995), Björk's *Homogenic* (1997), Nick Cave & The Bad Seeds' *The Boatman's Call* (1997), Massive Attack's *Mezzanine* (1998), Radiohead's *Kid A* (2000), along with too many hip-hop classics to mention and many others you can think of that are just not quite the same listening experiences across two sides of vinyl. These albums were native to the CD and better for it.

Music fans embraced CDs because of their novelty, convenience and *perceived* modernity. The mass penetration of CD players and persuasive tactics of music industry marketers drove us towards full-on replacement cycle consumption. But as a result, we listened to more albums than ever (well, we certainly *bought* more copies of more albums than ever). Album releases increased steadily in line with CD sales, the music industry more than happy to feed the beast. Album site Discogs estimated that some 318,576 titles were released in 1999 — more than triple the number in 1990. To help navigate these oppressive volumes, "best of" lists from the music press (and music journalism's new format, music blogs) became more important and, in symbiosis, made albums more central to popular culture, much more so than individual songs. Likewise, industry award shows seemed to get bigger and bigger, with new ones — like the Mercury Music Prize in the UK — cropping up with an air of the intellectual, discerning music fan, again helping raise the album's standing as a cultural good.

In short, the CD did the album no major harm. Eventually, however, it became a victim of its own success. By the time Napster rendered songs as music files, available for free, it gave many previous CD buyers the excuse they had been waiting for — to claim that "The music industry has been ripping us off for years." With prices peaking at £15, they were not wrong. It was payback time. I remember visiting Toronto for a music conference in 2002 and seeing a Canadian friend, whom I'd met when I was a computer programmer, before I got into the music business. He had mercilessly ripped his entire CD collection into MP3s and then sold off all the original copies. When I witnessed that, I knew it was the beginning of the end for the CD.

There were just too many bad albums. "All filler, no killer" reviews were commonly assigned by critics and fans. Sometimes, fawning reviews succumbed to the hype, but music fans were vexed when we heard the results. Yes, I'm talking about Oasis's *Be Here Now* and Blur's *The Great Escape* among far too many other album's that we didn't really need. The CD album purchase had become a lazy and unfulfilling habit — or a hazardous risk in which you were increasingly likely to get ripped off and purchase something you would instantly regret on playback: that sickening feeling that you had been duped by the business and that it might be time to give up on that band. The CDs biggest crime against the album was to puff it up, make it lazy and expensive, like some indulgent, over-entitled, faded rock star. The average CD collection included a fair proportion of discs only ever played just once.

Unfeasibly, the music industry still had designs on driving yet more replacement cycle consumption. But format wars, a cynical record buying public and weaker product arguments all round saw these attempts ultimately fall flat. The "super audio" CD (if you can believe that), DVD Audio and the minidisc were briefly hyped and even more swiftly despatched to obsolescence.

While a fair few legacy artists have had their run-ins with the music industry over the years, usually accusing labels of complacency (especially if their latest albums were left floundering), they might want to think twice. Sure, they may have signed a bad deal, and labels had got rich and lazy off of their backs, but had they released records themselves, would they have managed to sell the same songs three or four times over? They were about to do the same thing again — only this time, in perpetuity.

Chapter 3
Digital music and the dismantling of the disc

Sometime in 2005, I was being interviewed for CNN outside HMV, 194 Oxford Street. The UK's most respected music retailer had opened a shiny new store which featured digital music downloading stations, interactive listening posts, and even a small stage for in-store artist performances. HMV was aiming to modernise shopping, bravely placing new-world digital media alongside old-world physical formats, creating what it claimed to be then a new type of shopping experience and the largest record store in the world. In other branches, it had installed gaming stations and even juice bars. HMV was flying in the face of the prevailing trends away from physical record buying and towards both internet piracy and online shopping. By that time, even the first music streaming subscription service, Rhapsody, had launched. With the celestial jukebox now an earthly reality, who needed to go out to shop for music? The writing was on the wall for physical music, and the new flagship store turned out to be the latest in a string of dodgy decisions by the once-great retailer. In 1998, it had acquired a major book chain, Waterstones, which turned out to be a major distraction. It then stopped selling vinyl, assuming (reasonably) that the format was finally dead. In truth, HMV had begun to lose its way before digital music arrived on the scene. You couldn't blame them for trying to reposition their stores as a "third space" — it worked for Starbucks. But dropping in for a £3 cup of coffee every day was a better business than browsing entertainment options you could get in abundance from your laptop once you got to work.

For the interview, I towed the music industry line and talked about how the move demonstrated the rude health and ongoing resilience of not just physical formats but also brick and mortar retail. I, of course, believed nothing of the sort. I was saying one thing but thinking another — that this was a stupid mistake, doomed to fail within a year or two. As it turned out, the store lasted until 2019, finally closing when HMV fell into administration. It spent a few years lying empty, although for a brief time it was occupied by the parasitic American Candy, which colonised other decaying iconic buildings and was not a great look for London's West End.

For a long time before the closure, HMV had been a shadow of its former self, a lame dog limping along on the sales of DVD video and games, along with discounted books and low-end consumer electronics — and overpriced music CDs. The glory days of catering to a steady flow of "fifty-quid blokes" and music aficionados were long gone, and a visit to the store was a dispiriting experience for anyone with a previous notion as to what HMV had represented.

HMV / American Candy (photo by the author)

However, in an unexpected turn of events, HMV's flagship store at 363 Oxford Street was reopened in 2023, led by the vinyl resurgence and, against all odds, an uptick in CD sales. HMV's new owner was Putman Investments, a billion-dollar Canadian retail conglomerate that owns numerous retail chains, including toys and home stores. As the store reopened, Doug Putman claimed that "CDs had regained appeal because they were now relatively cheap and that there was also a 'doubling down on trying to buy everything [a band] comes out with'".[10] Whether the age of the music format chaser has returned to the extent that major music retailers can make a sustained comeback seems doubtful,

10 The *Guardian*, Mark Sweney and Sarah Butler, Friday 24 Nov 2023.

although the word "superfan" has been buzzing around the music industry for a few years now.

When record labels start to give up on a format, you know it's the endgame. Around the time HMV launched its shiny new multimedia megastore at Oxford Street, I was in the office of a senior music executive at EMI, up on the third floor of the plush atrium building on Wrights Lane (now home to major-label rival Warner Music). It was still the early days of digital music, and I was putting together the second edition of the IFPI's "Digital Music Report", in my then role as Research Director at the global trade body for the record labels. The report aimed to demonstrate that the music industry was at the cutting edge of innovation and was ready to embrace digital technology, but was really a puff piece suggesting the industry wasn't on its last legs, as much of the world's business press were reporting at the time. Truth was, no business reporter would have been convinced had they taken regular walks around the offices of record labels, in which CDs were still scattered about everywhere — piled high on desks, in boxes beside desks and, in the case of this particular executive, stacked tightly on wall-to-wall shelves all around the desk. But this guy was one of the smart ones.

"Take a look at that," he said, nodding towards those shelves, "a travesty of plastic." Well, he was right about that. By now, the CD had become an ugly duckling, packaged in the little clear plastic jewel case that chipped and faded at the edges in a deeply unflattering way — nothing like a dignified, well-worn vinyl sleeve, but more like something screaming to be taken to the dump. I responded with a short statement about how it was incumbent on the industry — namely the labels — to not surrender to the march of the MP3 but to innovate around the CD format to protect its category value.

This could be by way of a complete switch from the jewel case to the alternative "Digipak" (essentially a more durable plastic back with a paper-based booklet-style front), or added bonus digital content to help integrate physical and digital formats together as one. These were all ideas I believed in and advocated for on a daily basis at the time. The executive didn't stop for one second to consider any of this. Instead, he picked up a CD from a small pile on the edge of his desk and pitched it violently against the wall. It whizzed past my head. I was stunned into silence until I could finally utter, "Or maybe not." As we continued on with the business at hand — crafting confident quotes about the music industry's optimistic digital future, he apologised for the gesture, adding a final remark on the CDs future: "It's too late."

He was right. HMV might have launched what was the world's biggest record store, but by 2005 the music industry's biggest format was effectively as good as dead. The funeral had been arranged. CD sales began to decline year-on-year from 2001, but by 2004 the decline began steepening irreversibly. In 2004, over two billion CDs were shipped worldwide. By 2015, this number had plummeted to 569 million units — a decline of more than 70%. The problem wasn't so much the disc itself as the rapidly disappearing ways in which one could play it. Home hi-fi systems were being replaced by Bluetooth speakers. The iPod ruled, a new model being introduced every six months and the product range available in an increasing array of options — the "Touch", "Mini" and "Nano". Apple's music player would achieve peak sales just a few years later, in 2008, shifting 54.8 million units. Car manufacturers were beginning to talk about the idea of new cars without CD players (though it would take another six years before Ford ran a CD-less car off the production line). Mostly, the music industry had begun to give up on the format. The last hurrah for the CD had been the Universal Music "innovation" the "Super Jewel Box" in 2003. This updated design was positioned as a "reboot" of the CD and was intended to begin to replace the standard CD jewel case (provided rival labels went along with it, which, of course, they did not). The Super Jewel Box was a more durable and "aesthetically refined" package, with rounded edges, a stronger hinge and improved locking mechanisms to better protect discs from being chipped, battered and cracked. The problem was it was still ugly as hell. Besides, a packaging innovation by one record label, even the market leader, was almost guaranteed to be snubbed by the others. While it was adopted for some titles (as previously noted, for Universal's reissued Queen catalogue from 2011, released after the bands rights had transferred from the crumbling EMI a few years later), it never fully replaced the standard jewel case.

It was a beleaguered EMI that had one of the last major successes with the CD. In 2009, two years before Universal released those Queen remasters, EMI reissued the entire Beatles catalogue, each of the famous albums remastered in both stereo and mono mixes — with each release packaged in a luxurious Digipak, replicating the vinyl artwork of the original albums. Critics praised the remastering team for the enhanced sound, respecting the original recordings while improving dynamics and resolving technical imperfections. The project was seen as a major upgrade for a well-known catalogue, and by the end of 2009, sales had exceeded seventeen million units globally. Several Beatles albums re-entered charts around the world, including the UK and the US. Both the stereo and limited-edition mono box sets sold out quickly. Really, the success came down to EMI respecting those records as albums, keeping them as close as possible to their original form — just in miniature. The company refused to be seduced by the idea of going too far with digital release gimmicks (although the albums were made available on iTunes, Amazon and later on streaming platforms too). The success of The Beatles remasters preceded a major wave of similar projects by the major labels, including Pink Floyd, Led Zeppelin, Queen, David Bowie and The Rolling Stones. If the CD was on its way out, the labels could at least squeeze the last drops of profit from what had been the music industry's most profitable format ever, until streaming came along.

As the digital music era dawned, recording industry executives were most concerned about the death of the album.

The launch of iTunes in 2003 introduced the idea that music fans could now buy individual songs instead of full albums for the first time. Not only was this a clear gutting of the industry's biggest cash cow, but it also created havoc for the singles market. Unintended consequences included the most popular album tracks now entering and sometimes dominating the charts. Thus began a continuous engineering of chart eligibility rules — a constant, dull headache for the industry's trade bodies and chart committees.

Now that fans could cherry-pick the best songs instead of paying for ten to eighteen tracks, album sales began to tank, with the format itself suffering an identity crisis. Many artists, especially classic rock acts, saw iTunes as devaluing the artistic statement of an album and took on the role for themselves of defenders of the faith. Thus began the first wave of "digital holdouts". It was music industry politicking and a very messy business.

Metallica, already famous for confronting Napster in the early 2000s, also resisted iTunes initially. Drummer Lars

Ulrich: "The album format matters… we don't want our music chopped up into pieces." But Metallica had used up considerable energy taking up the fight with Napster, and their fans were already ripping their CDs onto iPods. Warner Music pushed them to embrace iTunes to stay competitive — the industry had changed, and digital music was now too big to ignore. By 2006, Metallica tracks could be unbundled.

Pink Floyd held out for longer. The band fought a legal battle against EMI in 2010, demanding that their albums not be sold as individual tracks on iTunes. Pink Floyd's contract with EMI (signed in 1999) prohibited the label from selling their music as separate tracks, preserving the band's album-oriented artistic vision. When EMI ignored this restriction and sold individual Pink Floyd songs on iTunes, the band sued, arguing that their albums were meant to be heard in full, not broken into pieces. Remarkably, the High Court ruled in Pink Floyd's favour, forcing EMI to pay damages. Just a year later, EMI was purchased by Universal Music Group, and Pink Floyd renegotiated their deal, and then allowed individual track sales. AC/DC held out for even longer. The band refused to put their music on iTunes, again insisting their albums should be consumed as a whole. Guitarist Angus Young said: "We don't make singles; we make albums." They didn't appear on iTunes until 2012, nearly a decade after its launch.

The undisputed heavyweights of the holdout, however, were Sheffield rockers Def Leppard. To those more rock-musically inclined, the Def Leppard digital story is fairly well known. The band first held out against iTunes, citing their belief, once again, in albums as full experiences (artist sentiment has held strong on this specific area as opposed to their executive counterparts, who were blindsided by the tech power players like Steve Jobs). The band's right to control its catalogue became a bone of contention, leading to a full scale falling-out with their label, Universal Music, which singer Joe Elliott described thus: "We just found out how offensive it was to have these people as our 'partners'. We're not going to let the enemy dictate our terms."

After the dispute, Def Leppard attempted to re-record some of their catalogue, so as to assert their copyright control, starting with the *Hysteria* album. But lightning doesn't strike twice. When you've cut a classic that took everything you had (and was counted by producer Mutt Lange as his best work), it's highly unlikely you'll recapture that magic again. Def Leppard probably knew it and, in the end, kept their re-recordings to just three underwhelming tracks. Def Leppard fangirl Taylor Swift had much more success with the same strategy many years later. But she had far greater marketing savvy than the luddite lads from Yorkshire.

Leppard withheld their digital rights, including from Spotify, up until January 2018, when they settled their dispute with Universal and struck a new deal. It's incredible to think that *Hysteria* landed on streaming services a full ten years into the streaming era, but over thirty years after its release. A fair few anniversary moments got missed there, then. Sometime in 2017, I was in attendance at a management conference at Spotify where, as part of the event, uber pop songwriter and human hit machine Max Martin was interviewed by then CEO Daniel Ek. It was fascinating to hear Max's take on everything about the art and commerce of the song, but towards the end of that conversation, the quietly spoken Martin turned the tables on Ek and became the interviewer: "I have a question for you actually… what the fuck happened to Def Leppard?" One could see the picture zapping through

Ek's mind of an audibly challenged big game cat but, ever cool and never flustered, he simply glanced the question off into the audience of… let's call them "music-tech execs". Of course, no one had a clue.

Joe Elliott may have lost all respect for Universal Music at the time, but the world's largest label had come close to "locking" albums on iTunes in the first place. The unbundling crisis genuinely had music executives wrestling with the angels. I remember being asked by Universal's then global head of digital, Rob Wells, "Do you think we should lock albums?" I thought it was a preposterous idea, to try and put the cat back in the bag. "You can't do that!" was my answer then. But I think I was wrong. Had the labels stood for their artists and the integrity of the album as the body of work, they might have earned back the respect lost for their hapless response to Napster and file sharing. But at the time, it was one of those genuinely tough calls. Later, in 2007, then boss of Warner Music Edgar Bronfman Jr reflected, "We made a mistake by licensing single tracks instead of entire albums."

The industry discourse at the time became a debate about the relevance and role of the album and whether artists should eschew it altogether. The argument for this was that the album was a trap, a square peg in a round hole, and artists could now break out of the vicious cycle and be free to shake things up. At a panel conference in London, the celebrity music analyst Mark Mulligan predicted that "some artists will be album artists, but many will be singles artists". The above-mentioned Robb Wells said that digital music was just the incentive artists needed to make their albums better. On another panel, high-profile investment analyst Helen Smith suggested that shorter albums seemed like the sensible way through it all, and we would see a return of the "extended play" record, the EP. As it turned out, this was close to the mark… eventually. In the streaming era, the EP has become a common way for emerging artists to release their debut and for established artists to keep audiences warm between proper albums.

Ironically, soon after Bronfman's statement, iTunes itself suddenly warmed to the album format. It introduced the "iTunes LP", a digital "rebundle" of the tracks, with animated album art, special bonus content, digital artwork and liner notes. This was Apple's attempt to make digital albums feel "deluxe" — like classic vinyl records with gatefold sleeves and inserts. A select few high-profile releases got the iTunes LP treatment, including The Beatles' remastered *Abbey Road*, Pink Floyd's *Dark Side of the Moon* and David Bowie's *The Rise And Fall Of Ziggy Stardust And The Spiders From Mars: 40th Anniversary Edition*. New releases on the format included Coldplay's *Viva La Vida or Death and All His Friends,* Daft Punk's *Random Access Memories* and Kanye West's *My Beautiful Dark Twisted Fantasy*.

The concept was well intended but had some obvious limitations. For one thing, it only worked on the desktop version of iTunes, not on the iPhones or the iPod. It was also prohibitively expensive. Priced between $15 and $20, it looked like a vanity purchase in a digital world where music was still available for free, and streaming services had entered the market with an all-you-can-eat model of music consumption. But the format was also costing Apple so much to produce that each release made a loss. The iTunes LP was no game-changer. It was more a case of Apple throwing the record labels a bone of appeasement — something the big tech players do every so often just to give the labels something to chew over. Why in this case might Apple have had a change of heart with the iTunes LP? The answer was the rapid encroachment of a little green monster. One that was about to get much, much bigger.

Meanwhile, the album's identity crisis deepened, and some artists decided it was time to break rank. This was no time to attempt to swim against the tide, but perhaps it was a chance to rage against the industry machine and, just maybe, keep hold of some semblance of a fanbase. Irish rock band Ash declared the death of the album in 2007. After just five studio albums, the band retired the format, saying they would only release singles from then on. They instead blazed a trail with "The A to Z Series", releasing twenty-six singles in a row instead of a traditional album. Ash dropped one new song every two weeks between October 2009 and September 2010, keeping them simpatico with their fans and constantly connected to the music scene. Except it didn't work. Sales and chart performance were poor by the band's previous standards. The singles were bundled into two compilation albums, neither of which made any impact, other than to nudge the band's career in the wrong direction. By 2015, they went back on their decision, releasing *Kablammo!* as a full-length album. Tim Wheeler and crew learned their lesson. In tech entrepreneur language, "being early is as good as being wrong". Ash went back to the album, following up three years later with *Islands*, and released an impressive eighth album in 2024 called *Race The Night*. Ash doesn't play any of the A to Z songs in their live shows.

In 2009, Billy Corgan of our favourite album band of the CD era, The Smashing Pumpkins, said that the band was "done making albums" and that "The idea of making a traditional album doesn't fit the way people listen to music anymore." This time, Corgan conceived the new project *Teargarden by Kaleidyscope* as a forty-four-song series, releasing one track at a time for free on the band's website. The idea was to abandon the album cycle and make music an ongoing, constantly evolving process. The episodic song release would likely become the new standard for bands. Corgan described it as a return to the 1960s singles era, where every song was its own standalone event. It sounded right, except nobody paid attention for long. The *Teargarden* project started off well enough, but fans quickly lost track, and the scattered single drops didn't generate momentum. It's fair to say the project drifted, so much so that Corgan and the band got bored of their own idea. After releasing just ten out of the planned forty-four songs, Corgan shifted gears and compiled the next batch of songs into a full album: *Oceania* (2012). From there, it was all albums moving forward for The Smashing Pumpkins.

The "innovative" release strategies continued. The Kaiser Chiefs released the "episodic album". British singer-songwriter Nerina Pallot released a song a month throughout 2009. Again, nobody cared. The real problem with all the song projects was keeping hold of people's attention — ironically, the very problem that song makers thought they would solve. Individual songs, untethered from albums, just weren't that interesting. It was less like Billy Corgan's vision of a return to the jolly 1960s and more like a form of rationing for items nobody actually needed. It was like buying eggs one at a time from the supermarket. You couldn't do anything with them. The failed experiments proved that songs needed to be on albums, and that albums needed to land with a bang before fans would really care enough to be interested. This was especially true for bands like Ash and Smashing Pumpkins but applied pretty much to the artist community across the board. The gallop of the episodic song quickly reverted back to the slow walk of the periodic album. Whether the song-by-song initiatives had come too soon is an interesting theory. iTunes wasn't yet adept at data-driven recommendations, and playlists weren't "a thing". Indeed, iTunes was full of pretty awful "iMix" mixtapes that nobody carried any torches for. If artists had acted in unison and gone the way of songs only, chaos would have reigned. Which songs from the episodic releases can you name as your favourites? Exactly. The irony here is that even on the new unbundled music service, songs just had nowhere to go. They sat alongside each other as boring lists of titles, just like files in a spreadsheet. AC/DC, a fully paid-up, card-carrying member of the holdouts club, recognised this and — with tongues firmly in cheeks — released a music video as an actual spreadsheet.

Imagine what would have been lost with a permanent swing away from the album. Artists often talk about albums being a type of chain reaction, with new projects often bouncing off in a new direction away from the previous one. Those chain-reaction career arcs would have been totally lost. Albums are much more than the sum of their parts in a way that songs cannot ever manage, no matter how they are alternatively packaged. Albums have come in pairs, companion sets, as with *Folklore* and *Evermore*. This was a deliberate throwback to other classic pairings such as *Kid A* and *Amnesiac*. There have been classic trilogies, such as David Bowie's 1970s Berlin trio of albums — *Low*, *Heroes* and *Lodger* — something The Weeknd emulated with his previous three albums: *After Hours*, *Dawn FM* and *Hurry Up Tomorrow*. The album stands for so much in terms of artistry, as well as how we receive music, digest it and reflect upon it. Famous albums receive as much post-analysis as the most celebrated novels, movies and works of art. As listeners, we often see the artists we follow as passing through distinct career phases, almost always defined by the albums they made at the time — whether it's The Cure's "dark trilogy of the 1980s" (*Seventeen Seconds, Faith* and *Pornography*) or Kanye West's transformative set of albums (*808s & Heartbreak, My Beautiful Dark Twisted Fantasy, Yeezus*) between 2008 and 2013.

My personal favourite is to think of the journey of U2 from 1987 to 1993. These are "my" U2 years, in which they transformed from the grandiose Americana of *The Joshua Tree* to the European alternative, industrial pop of *Achtung Baby* in 1991 and then on to the lighter, experimental "post-genre" pop of 1993's *Zooropa*. Over the course of three albums, the band fearlessly expanded its repertoire and found a sense of humour in the process. But I know other U2 fans who see it differently and would instead group together their grand rock period of 1984–1988, *The Unforgettable Fire*, *The Joshua Tree* and *Rattle and Hum*. Or indeed, the shift to more experimental ground across the next three albums *Achtung Baby*, *Zooropa* and finally *Pop*, before the band returned to a more traditional sound. You can slice and dice U2 and any other famous band by sequences of albums in this way. Who knows, some U2 fans may even prefer their "later albums". Just don't dwell too long on U2s own unfortunate experiment with digital-only release strategies… as we'll note shortly.

After the failure of the episodic song release experiments, others had mixed success by doing something different but very much sticking with the album as the main vehicle. In 2007, Radiohead kicked up dust with its "pay-what-you-want" release, *In Rainbows,* but neither they nor any other artist repeated the trick. That same year, Nine Inch Nails' *Year Zero* was released as an "alternate reality game" with clues hidden in USB drives, websites, phone numbers and secret concerts. Fans had to decode messages to piece together a dystopian storyline. All of it eventually led to the band's sixth actual album. In 2011, Björk released ***Biophilia*** as the world's first "app album". Released as an interactive app with unique visuals and mini-games for each song, it received mixed reviews but niche adoption. Once again, there was no first-mover advantage for Björk, nor did anyone follow suit. ***Biophilia*** was less commercially successful than Björk's previous studio albums.

We return to U2 for the most underwhelming idea of the lot. It came a few years later, with U2's disastrous "hard-coded" iPhone album release for ***Songs of Innocence***, in 2014. Apple automatically added the album to five hundred million iTunes accounts without anyone's consent. Talk about misreading the room. The idea was so far off the mark that it has ended up at the very top of all the things Bono will keep apologising for as long as he lives. In his 2022 book, ***Surrender***, he states: "We had put a bottle of milk in people's fridge that they hadn't asked for. It was a serious overreach."

You have to admire the fact that Bono's apology drew some lineage from Paul Weller's legendary comment on the iPod being a "mini-fridge with no fucking beers in it". It is cold in them there Apple devices. To be fair to Apple, Bono also revealed that Apple executive Eddy Cue had warned him that auto-downloading the album could backfire, but Bono envisioned the project as a "philanthropic gift". Mercifully, it remains a unique take on the album.

Far more successful as an album release strategy on iTunes came courtesy of Beyoncé, who dropped her 2013 self-titled release as an entire album overnight on iTunes, with zero marketing. Somehow, Beyoncé had managed to keep the project's release under wraps despite the massive scale of the project, which included music videos for every track — creating a genuine first: the visual album. Fans and media went into a frenzy, making it one of the most successful surprise releases ever. Unlike the above examples, it instantly led to more artists wanting to do a surprise release. Beyoncé got it right. What made the difference was the simplicity of the idea — and yet the difficulty level too. When most were looking to "innovate" with gimmicks, Beyoncé zigged against the zags. And the album is great too. Probably under-appreciated at the time, *Beyoncé* was critical in both protecting and reinforcing the album. It swept away the gimmicky projects that had come before it, yet it embraced the idea that music had once again become as much about visuals as it had in the days of MTV.

2016, the year of the weaponised album

In 2016, Chance the Rapper's *Coloring Book* became the first streaming-exclusive album to win a Grammy as well as the first "DIY" album release to achieve mainstream success. However, this time there was a catch. *Coloring Book* was released exclusively on Apple Music for two weeks, a privilege for which Apple reportedly paid Chance $500,000. It was one of a series of Apple Music exclusives used as a competitive strategy against the rapidly ascending Spotify.

Throughout 2016, the album became an Apple Music weapon in the streaming wars. Travis Scott, Drake, Taylor Swift and Britney Spears were among some of the high-profile artists that allowed Apple Music a two-week exclusivity window on their album releases during 2016 in exchange for a one-off bonus pay-out. Apple saw it at the time as its most effective way to put the brakes on Spotify's runaway success train. It didn't do that, but it did ruffle Spotify's feathers. Had it retaliated with its own exclusives, music streaming platforms might look more like video streamers today, offering incomplete and competing content catalogues. Instead, Spotify played it cool — and got a stroke of luck, as the tactic came to an abrupt halt with Frank Ocean's *Blonde*.

Released on 20 August as an Apple Music exclusive, *Blonde* became one of the most notorious manoeuvres in music industry history. Ocean's deal with Def Jam/Universal had one album left on his contract. But Ocean wanted to be more like Chance the Rapper — to own his music and be a truly independent artist. So he delivered a visual album, *Endless* (an exclusive to Apple for the usual two weeks), to fulfil his Def Jam contract. It looked like he'd done a Beyoncé, but *Endless* wasn't a "proper" album. That came just a day later, in the form of *Blonde*, again exclusively on Apple Music. However, now out of contract, *Blonde* was self-released under Ocean's own label. The album was a sensational hit, reaching No. 1 on the Billboard charts while cutting Universal out of the picture. Ocean had pretty much tricked his way out of a major-label deal. Just days after the event, Universal CEO Lucian Grainge sent a memo to all Universal labels forbidding exclusive deals with Apple, Tidal or Spotify. When Universal makes a move like that, others follow, and the exclusive album window was closed for good. Overnight, Frank Ocean had effectively killed the Apple Music album exclusive, a massive stroke of good fortune for Spotify. The brakes were off.

By the time the iTunes album arrived in 2009, Spotify was still some way off reaching the inflection point that would kick the Swedish tech firm into hypergrowth. The streaming service kept on getting in its own way with innovations that didn't really work. Firstly, there was an integration with the UK-based MP3 download store 7Digital, which allowed users to buy and download MP3 tracks directly from the Spotify app. A "buy button" was placed next to songs, which redirected users to 7Digital. Given Spotify's committed streaming model, this was an uncertain move and, as a consumer offering, confusing. Then came the "Spotify App Finder", a built-in (desktop only) app store inside Spotify that allowed third-party developers to create music-related apps (a bit like a music version of the Apple App Store). Early apps included *Rolling Stone*, *Pitchfork*, Last.fm, Songkick concert recommendations and TuneWiki (lyrics). It looked like a game-changing innovation, but most Spotify users didn't catch on to using niche services such as *Pitchfork* reviews. Then came "Discover", a premature attempt at dynamic feed of real-time personalised song recommendations based on collaborative filtering technology. Again, it fell flat. It was all too clever, yet at the same time not quite smart enough. Besides, the tech world was switching from the computer to the mobile phone and Spotify badly needed to declutter its user experience. Spotify was learning the hard way, through a series of failed experiments, that what was really needed was something far simpler.

The answer — ironically, for a super-smart, data-driven tech company — was to think much more like a traditional music company. The answer was Today's Top Hits. Spotify had begun to hire people from the music business into an in-house editorial team, including former MTV editor Tuma Basa and music researcher Doug Ford, who had worked for playlist app Tunigo, which had previously been acquired by Spotify. The Spotify Editorial team launched a series of genre playlists that, once placed prominently on the app's homepage, took off like a rocket. After all the weird tech, it was old-fashioned editorial taste-makers that found Spotify's sweet spot with its users.

Within the space of eighteen months — from the beginning of 2014 to the summer of 2015 — Today's Top Hits, Hot

Country, RapCaviar, Baila Reggaeton and others had become replacement radio for younger listeners, and Spotify *the* place to discover new music. Before long, the in-house curated playlists had enough combined followers to have a major direct influence on the tracks that were featured on the music charts — still the music industry's primary bellwether of success. If Spotify added a song, its streams skyrocketed, helping artists break into the Billboard Hot 100 and other music charts around the world. Those playlists made Spotify a power player in the music industry, with label executives falling over themselves to get their artists featured.

Building on the momentum, Spotify also had its first significant success with algorithmic playlists, the form of Discover Weekly, which launched in the summer of 2015. A personalised playlist of thirty songs that refreshed every Monday, Discover Weekly was the first major algorithm-driven playlist that delivered results that impressed listeners. Within a year, over forty million users had tried Discover Weekly, and many of them made the playlists a regular feature. For the industry, it helped break new artists, with independent and lesser-known musicians getting featured alongside the big names. It was a transformational step in music discovery — so much so that Spotify began to see music discovery as its main strength and even its central purpose. Indeed, it paved the way for more algorithmic-playlist brands such as Release Radar and Daily Mix.

Spotify's in-house playlists drained all promotional power from traditional radio, smashed what was left of iTunes and killed off the last remnants of physical music retail everywhere. Suddenly, the album was missing in action. As playlists dominated the music landscape, the album began to look dangerously irrelevant, a true anachronism. I thought so myself. I had launched my own playlist site and, in a blog for MIDiA Research in 2019, I wrote that

> It strikes me as high time the industry now evaluates just what a 'post-album' world will look and sound like. So perhaps somewhere to start is to think about more innovation with the format that in essence, has replaced the album - playlists.

Although playlists changed the way we listen more than they changed music itself, the irrepressible crush to get a song added to a playlist also began to affect the way songs were written, produced and mixed. Music marketers wanted "streaming hits" and a savvy troupe of independent and younger pop artists began making "Spotify Core", songs made to a precision-tooled formula of structure and sounds designed to avoid being skipped, so that they would perform relatively well on playlists. Spotify Core was a genre lacking in nuance, but it was ear candy — instantly catchy and with an ability to crowd out other, less immediate types of music, including songs written for albums.

The music industry had become a brutal, Darwinian ecosystem where only the (Spotify Core) song survived. The whole industry became hyper-focused on making songs for playlists, getting songs added to playlists and doing their best to avoid the song being removed from playlists. The scale of this obsession cannot be overstated. The topic dominated almost every marketing discussion in the music business in the latter half of the 2010s. Labels pushed artists to release constant singles instead of waiting for full albums, adapting to streaming's song-economy revenue model. Artists and music industry executives essentially became prisoners of playlists.

In this new environment, what chance did songs that played the role of "album tracks" have, be they either an essential part of the album's story or, indeed, filler between the hits?

In truth, playlists succeeded because they more closely reflected the way consumers now interacted with music. Aficionados and music tastemakers spent time making playlists, compiling and selecting songs and sharing them with others. It was mixtape culture on steroids. But passive listeners were perfectly happy to fire up the app, hit play and go with the flow.

If the first port of call for music consumers was to hear songs on playlists, much of the context around the music was being lost. Consumer research showed that listeners were hard pushed to recall song titles, or identify the artists performing the song, let alone the albums those songs were taken from. Playlists inevitably got longer too. Discover Weekly and the big Spotify curated brands had initially converged at around thirty to fifty songs, but the number drifted ever higher, with playlists soon lasting for between three and ten hours, containers for hundreds of songs.

Despite this, remarkably, none of Spotify's streaming competitors had anything like the success of Spotify with playlists. Amazon, Apple and Deezer seemed to have largely no idea how to respond other than by playing follow-the-leader, launching their own playlists with similar themes, similar names and even virtually the same style of thumbnail visuals as those on Spotify. Attempts to innovate with something different were near to embarrassing. US streaming rival Pandora launched something called Stories, a muddled mesh of podcasts and playlists, which seemed more like a throwback to the old-style radio that playlists had just destroyed.

Meanwhile, Spotify's suite of in-house playlists, both curated, algorithmic and the in-between ones (called "algotorial") had become the company's unique competitive advantage. They were collectively referred to internally by Spotifyers as "owned and operated" (O&O) properties, as opposed to the millions of independent playlists including those offered by the major labels. The central strategy for Spotify became to drive as much "on-platform" consumption as possible through its "O&O" suite, thus having a direct and controllable influence on which music was most likely to succeed. Spotify was in clear position to prioritise its "O&O real estate" via its homepage, search results and recommendation algorithms — while, in the process, neutering the influence of the millions of other playlists posted on the platform by third parties. This was what Daniel Ek meant when he said that "we control the demand for music" in an early post-IPO investor presentation.

Albums didn't fit anywhere into this masterplan. As Spotify's playlists grew, the album's importance declined precipitously to the point where the album looked in danger of extinction. While playlists and Spotify's success brought the industry back to growth, artists and labels were becoming increasingly concerned about the power that Spotify wielded. Labels were in two minds. On the one hand, song growth was so powerful that it was time to stop caring about the impact on album profits and just enjoy the profits full stop. But the dilemma was whether or not to actively steer artists away from the idea of making albums altogether. The sentiment went roughly along the lines that "streaming doesn't kill albums, but it forces artists to stay relevant with continuous output".

Perhaps Robb Wells had been right: artists just needed to make their albums better — shorter, leaner, coherent and yes, probably more frequent. But for the most part, albums got longer too. The more tracks on the album, the more tracks were available to stream — all of which counted towards "album equivalent sales", which then counted towards a chart position. While it made no real sense to keep on counting "album sales" when both albums and sales were dead in the water, the music industry did it anyway. This stubborn and byzantine practice turned out to be a lifeline for the album.

Spotify counts streams because that's what people do on Spotify. Of course, Spotify also knows when users listen through entire albums, but it doesn't tell anybody about that — perhaps because that type of listening on Spotify is extremely rare. If stream counts are the closest thing to a true measure of music listening, it begs the following question: If the music industry did the sensible thing and abandoned the fake construct of "album equivalent", would the album format itself collapse?

A stream counts as official after just thirty seconds. That's the basis on which Spotify and other streaming services report to label, artist, publisher and songwriter partners. After thirty seconds, that's when Spotify coughs up the small fractions of a cent. All of it on a per-song basis. The recording industry has refused to accept this when it comes to reporting its own industry performance, which it still aggregates to a form of "sales" reporting — an oxymoron in an era where music consumption is monetised via subscription payments. More bizarrely, however, the music industry stuck with the album as a unit when putting together these reports, even though whole-album streams are not reported by streaming services. This is like measuring the flat Earth after the discovery that it is in fact, round. For the UK market, one thousand streams under a paid, premium subscription service and six thousand ad-supported streams (on the free version of Spotify, the only streamer remaining with a free-to-use option) are aggregated across *any or all of the tracks on a particular album releas*e to arrive at the "album equivalent". The Entertainment Retailers Association (ERA) reported that 201 million such album equivalents were consumed in the UK in 2024. Music journalist Eamonn Forde, writing in the *Guardian* in January 2024, said that this system of "conflating streams and sales is like trying to amalgamate clouds and concrete". A closer analogy might be a look across to the video industry and Netflix. The on-demand video streamer notoriously does not even report any data to video or film industry bodies, so the video industry has no choice but to accept the reality that streaming is streaming, a form of consumption that is essentially beyond counting in units. Spotify relates to Netflix more than it does to the music industry. Both operate "engagement model" businesses. Just like any social media platform, they eventually profit from taking up our time. As such, measuring time is a metric of greater value to Spotify than the stream counts it relays to its music business partners. The time users spend on the app equates directly to engagement with it, and therefore the value placed on it, making users more likely to continue to subscribe rather than churn.

The music industry runs on a different model. Despite the fact that music is essentially sound waves, the industry has always sold packaged products and could not readjust its structure to match the engagement model. As things turned out, that's a good thing, because time spent on Spotify doesn't necessarily mean time listening to music. Indeed, as Spotify seems to have plotted from very early on, music takes up an ever decreasing share amongst many other forms of content on the platform. It could be time listening to, or watching, an increasingly dizzying choice of audio podcasts, audiobooks, video podcasts and, most recently, video tutorials or courses on anything from how to potty train your toddler whilst doing yoga to Dr Rangan Chatterjee's *A Blueprint for Healthy Living*. Spotify is now a pocket library (or perhaps more like YouTube). In the relentless drive for engagement, data-driven recommendations based on music tastes have become secondary to serving up videos about matching tattoos or the latest podcast on football or politics.

Here's the issue for the music business: as music takes up a declining share of engagement time on the big tech platforms, those same platforms have increasingly become the predominant way music is consumed. This means that the music business needs those platforms more than vice versa. It's ironic, because Spotify and its competitors could never have existed without music in the first place.

Streaming comprised around 85% of the total UK recorded music market in 2024, while physical sales made up 13%, and downloads the remainder. So vinyl, CD and cassettes only make up 13% of the market by value. Is that enough to shore up the album? The OCC launched the Official Vinyl Albums Chart in 2015 and the world's other top five music markets — the USA, Germany, France and Japan — followed suit. As physical formats return to critical mass, real album sales could stand up on their own and might be a truer reflection of which artists are succeeding in the world of album culture, as opposed to muddying the waters with "album equivalent" stream counts.

The album chart, as it stands, reflects both a more niche consumption culture and a more plentiful supply of music. With ever-higher release volumes and front-loaded marketing campaigns designed around getting the coveted No. 1, some forty-five albums reached the UK album chart top spot in 2024 (and for thirty-four of those, *physical* music formats accounted for the majority of first-week sales). Back in 1990, with fewer releases reaching more music buyers, just nineteen albums reached the No. 1 position. A No. 1 album is still impressive, especially in today's flooded market. Certainly, the music industry believes so from a marketing standpoint. The No. 1 album spot has become more coveted than ever, but why? After all, music fans no longer seem to care whether an artist goes big on the charts or not.

It's down to badges. A No. 1 record remains important to artists, even if it is a vanity measure compared with the album's imperious years. A record label can use a No. 1 album as a byline for an extended promotional campaign. Artist managers, meanwhile, use the No. 1 album as a bargaining chip with live agents and promoters, leveraging a higher spot on a festival bill or a step up in venue size on the touring circuit.

The growing importance of vinyl to music fans (and of the album charts to the music industry) has come at a time when the song economy has gone to another level altogether. In November 2018, then unknown rapper Lil Nas X released "Old Town Road", a "country-rap" song that blew up on TikTok and subsequently on music streaming services. By March 2020, the song hit No. 1 on the Billboard Hot 100, where it stayed for nineteen weeks. Songs had entered a new phase, becoming "short-form content" on social media, making it easy for users to engage with music through dance trends, challenges and memes. Tracks could explode overnight without music marketers pushing any buttons at all. Algorithms prioritised discovery, meaning older or lesser-known songs could suddenly trend, giving new life to catalogue music. When Fleetwood Mac's "Dreams" was used in one (now infamous) video clip on TikTok, the music industry realised that music could find its way to a new audience at any time in its life, unconnected from when it was released. Music suddenly had no time stamp. Music was new if it was "new to you".

The success of TikTok in surfacing music to vast audiences knocked Spotify for six. When Spotify awoke from an extended nap during the COVID-19 pandemic, it found that playlists were not only no longer flavour of the month, they were also hardly mentioned in casual conversation any more. Music marketers quickly switched their route one obsession away from playlists to TikTok videos. They began spending their marketing budgets on seeding content to social media influencers and boosting user-generated clips in the hope of going viral.

While music marketers chased after viral videos and A&R executives scoured TikTok for new talent, artists kept their focus on making albums — particularly albums that might gain cultural traction. This shift was led by a crop of mainly female solo artists looking to do things differently but also take the art of music making seriously. Rather than wait to be asked to jump through the usual hoops to promote their records, artists like Lana Del Rey, FKA twigs, Billie Eilish, Lizzo, Ariana Grande and Rosalia did what Beyoncé had done with her self-titled album of 2013 and ripped up the music marketer's rulebook. For 2019's *Norman Fucking Rockwell*, Lana Del Rey did minimal mainstream promotion but instead held poetry readings and a few small intimate gigs. The album's cover art, a striking photo of the artist with the model Duke Nicholson (as usual shot by Del Rey's sister Chuck Grant) was teased at museums and galleries, making it feel like a work of pop art. Meanwhile FKA twigs signalled her new album *Magdalene* through surreal, avant-garde visuals, rather than traditional singles. She performed pole-dance routines as part of her live shows and used high-art collaborations with photographer Matthew Stone to signal her as a visionary artist, not just a musician. These examples inspired other artists to take the high ground. As the COVID-19 pandemic took hold, it seemed as if people might have the attention spans not just for reading classics and watching old box sets, but also for listening to albums while the homemade bread was baking in the oven. More albums, even those more challenging to listen to, hit a cultural nerve. With its themes of trauma, isolation and female empowerment, Fiona Apple's *Fetch the Bolt Cutters* was not designed for radio play or individual hits, but was an experimental, free-flowing narrative that feels like a single performance. Taylor Swift's *Folklore* dropped as a surprise release and marked a new direction for the artist who would then dominate the global pop scene for years to come. Suddenly, the world's biggest and most popular artists were doubling down on the album as an artistic statement — even in an era dominated by TikTok-fuelled singles. The job of artists, arguably, is to work against the grain, and by 2021, artists shifted their own priorities towards projects with strong themes, concepts and cohesive visuals. This was when Adele, having spent five years making her third album, *30*, decided that enough was enough and requested that Spotify remove the default shuffle button, reinforcing that albums should be played in sequence.

By 2021, the album had pushed its way back into the cultural narrative. Vinyl had achieved a critical mass, and perhaps, post-COVID-19, consumers were a little more receptive to its throwback qualities. Albums like *30* and *Folklore* were such big records as to give a sense of the pre-digital era, when big albums were events in themselves. A new generation of avant-garde yet popular artists like Billie Eilish and Doja Cat built narratives across their albums. The world's biggest streaming star, The Weeknd, released *Dawn FM*, a full concept album with a narrative about existentialism. Kanye West's *Donda* and Lil Nas X's *Montero* had similar significance. For their thematic bodies of work, artists wanted vinyl pressings — preferably with a variety of colourways and special editions. Playlists and viral videos? If they happened, then great, but the album was the centrepiece.

In November 2023, *Billboard* ran a piece entitled "They Said the Album Was Dying. They Were Wrong",[11] which highlighted how other major US acts such as Zach Bryon, Rod Wave and Peso Pluma were also achieving huge success through primarily focusing on albums "that listeners engage with from start to finish" and building their campaigns around the idea of encouraging fans to participate in the artist's world more deeply. Not least, these artists and their marketing teams were doing so in part because of the futility of constantly chasing viral success on TikTok.

In 2022, vinyl outsold CDs in the UK and US for the first time in decades, marking a symbolic shift in physical music consumption. The following year, vinyl became the highest-grossing physical music format worldwide for the first time since its final imperium of 1982. By the time 2024 came around, Taylor Swift had established herself as a giant of the album format. *The Tortured Poets Department* was the USA's best-selling vinyl album of 2024, shifting 1.5 million units (as reported by Luminate). The album found its way to fans via no less than six distinct vinyl editions, each one named after its own track and featuring unique artwork.

---

[11] Elias Leight, They Said the Album Was Dying. They Were Wrong, Billboard online, November 16th, 2023.

Swift's *The Tortured Poets Department* shifted over four times more than the next best-seller, Billie Eilish, whose fourth full-length album, *Hit Me Hard and Soft*, was her most commercially successful album so far. What both Swift and Eilish have in common is releasing their albums not with lead singles but by building anticipation for the projects with superfans, and then pushing beyond their fan bases into a broader cultural impact. In both cases, the focus is on the album rather than a particular song. In 2024, nine of the Top 10 selling vinyl albums sold in the US were by female solo artists: Swift (with five titles), Eilish, Sabrina Carpenter and Olivia Rodrigo. The other one was Fleetwood Mac's *Rumours*. The five most streamed artists on Spotify in 2024 were women: Swift, Eilish and Carpenter, along with Karol G and Ariana Grande. All five had huge success with their major album projects. The impact these artists have had on album culture — and on bringing the album to the attention of younger female audiences — cannot be underestimated.

Chapter 4
Record retail and the vinyl resurgence

It's a quiet Tuesday afternoon in February at my local record shop, Banquet Records. I've dropped by to pick up my copy of The Wombats' *Oh! The Ocean* LP, which I had bought as part of a "ticket bundle". My daughters got the other half of the bargain: seeing the band play at the Pryzm nightclub. As I take to browsing the indie isle (I'm accepting that I'm duty bound to leave the shop with at least one other title under my arm), a Spanish lady in her middle years is asking one of the staff about "something modern" from the jazz section, as a gift for her husband. The staffer, despite his opening caveat that jazz "is not my genre", is right on it. His recommendations are spot on. Mercury Prize and BRITs winners Ezra Collective's *Where I'm Meant To Be* gets top billing, but another recommendation is Kamasi Washington's *Fearless Movement* — and I am somewhat more impressed than the Spanish lady. I can't help but intervene and point out that behind them, on the main wall display, are two fine examples of modern classics: Nubya Garcia's *Odyssey* and Yussef Dayes's *Black Classical Music* (though both are pricey special editions). This one short conversation in a record shop is already suggestive of what an incredibly rich seam of talent runs through whatever we might call "modern jazz". The Spanish lady changes tack and asks for something perhaps "more classic". She buys a copy of Miles Davis's *Kind of Blue*. Both I and the shop assistant are thinking the same thing, that if the husband is a jazz fan, it may be unlikely he is not one of the twenty-five million people who own a copy of *Kind of Blue*. Then again, if he is not yet a jazz fan, he soon should be, since his wife has found him the best entryway into the world of jazz ever recorded. And another copy is sold. *Kind Of Blue* was first released in 1959, but has since been rereleased in a new format, remastered version or special edition package more times than any other jazz record. I wonder if, in sixty years' time, people will still wander into record shops and come out with a copy of *Kind of Blue*. You have to say, it is *probable*. While I'm in the shop, there are three other customers. One fits the classic profile of the vinyl record shopper — a white man dressed just a few years younger than his middle-aged self. The other two are, generically speaking, "youth". This is the future of record shopping. In his essay "For the Love of Records", David Hepworth wrote: "We love the sound of music as much as we ever did but our emotions are no longer triggered by proximity to the vessels that carry it... Soon those feelings will be gone from our culture entirely." It was a logical, almost forgone conclusion when he published this in 2018. But by the miraculous and illogical nature of our love for music, it turned out not to be true. Every time I visit a record shop now, I see young people milling around, on both sides of the counter. And I see the excited anticipation on the faces of those walking away from the counter with their square carrier bag. It gives me hope for music that young people will spend £25 on something they can get to hear for free, and that this is trending upwards. We don't have to be old to want to appreciate music as an affordable luxury.

I leave with my Wombats record and a copy of the Manic Street Preachers' new LP, *Critical Thinking*. It was a spontaneous purchase, though de-risked by several listens on Spotify and the knowledge that The Manics are on a good run.

Another successful, nourishing but restrained trip to Banquet Records. This local independent record shop might serve a diverse profile of fairly local punters, but it is unique in that it also attracts top artists from all over the globe to Kingston Upon Thames, an otherwise nondescript suburban shopping town. Here, at the sticky-floored Pryzm nightclub (on the town's busy ring road next to a bowling alley and Odeon cinema complex) artists play intimate live sets to a mix of hard-core fans and local residents, as well as drop into the Banquet shop on Eden Street for album signings and meet-and-greets. Artists from Michael Bublé to Ed Sheeran to Charli XCX, and bands from Suede to Pale Waves to Interpol have dropped by in recent times. The reason an independent record shop can attract significant global music stars is that the economics work. Ticket sales mean the shows break even, but because they are bundled with either a vinyl or CD purchase, the artist gets to make some real money. By selling two hundred vinyl records at £30 each, an artist can make somewhere between one and two thousand pounds from royalties in a day. To make the same amount of cash on Spotify, they would need to notch up a couple of *million* streams. That might take a while longer. The real deal-maker, however, is that the ticket/album bundle sales count significantly towards the UK album charts. A remarkable two in five artists to have landed a No. 1 album in the UK in 2024 had played live at one of Banquet's five small venues in Kingston: Pryzm, two churches, a local boozer and the shop itself (since refurbished and rebranded as Circuit). This led the *New Statesman* to name Banquet "the unofficial kingmaker of the UK album chart". Hence, seeing a luxury tour bus parked up outside the shabby Pryzm is now a common sight. It has taken Banquet Records a decade to get to this point, but the cultural impact of this otherwise small business is a significant win for independent record shops.

Wherever they are located around the world, indie record stores are staging small in-store events, serving gourmet coffee and an old fashioned sense of community. Music on the high street is going beyond just record stores. In some cities, music retail is morphing with the food, beverage and hospitality sector to create "music bars" in which the listening experience is as central to the proposition as a cocktail or glass of wine. Since the 1950s, Tokyo and Kyoto have been famous for Jazz "kissa" and vinyl bars, with some recently becoming sensations on — you guessed it — Instagram. The trend has recently spread to global cultural centres like London, New York and Berlin, which host a crop of newer music bars with high-end sound systems.

The increasing influence of independent record stores on the music industry in the 2020s is one of the music business's quieter success stories. ERA reported that there were 471 indie record stores operating in the UK in 2024, an increase of almost one hundred from the 375 recorded in 2020. Some 2.6 million vinyl records were sold through indie stores, with 39% of total UK vinyl album sales. Over in the US, Luminate also reported that the same proportion of vinyl sales went through indie stores there in 2024.

But it's not just independent and specialist music shops that have grown alongside the vinyl boom. HMV returned to its old address in London's Oxford Street, for the second time. The iconic Tower Records relaunched in 2020, albeit as an online retailer. In 2024, the UK's Our Price took the same route.

In 2016, UK supermarket chain Sainsbury's reintroduced vinyl records to its stores after a thirty-year absence. Other supermarkets — including Tesco and, later, Asda — followed suit, though with mixed success (the big supermarket chains have since begun a retreat from selling music). That didn't stop beleaguered UK stationary and bookseller WH Smith stocking vinyl records in 2024 (in eighty of its five hundred high-street shops). Within a year, however, WH Smith had gone under, its stores taken over by Modella Capital. Whether the (inexplicably branded) TGJones stores will stock vinyl remains to be seen.

By now, however, vinyl had gone so mainstream as to warrant being added back on to the list of products used to calculate UK inflation. None other than John Lewis, the UK's most middle-of-the-road department store, began selling vinyl in February 2025. John Lewis partnered with indie music retailer Rough Trade to offer a "curated selection" of vinyl records in select department stores as well as online. The important thing here is that if the "mainstreaming" of vinyl continues, so too will the format's growth — at a point where many in the music industry feel like vinyl sales must be on the verge of peaking.

The Recording Industry Association of America (RIAA) reported that vinyl sales increased for the eighteenth straight year in 2024, selling forty-four million and reaching \$1.4 billion, the highest level since 1984 and 8% of the total value of the recorded music business in the US. In the UK, vinyl album sales reached a thirty-year high in 2024, with 6.7 million units and £196 million, just over 8% of the value of UK recorded music revenues. It was the seventeenth consecutive year of growth for the format, but the fifth year straight of double-digit growth. In value terms, vinyl has kept up the pace with music streaming.

Underpinning vinyl's new growth are far more younger record buyers. Even though they didn't grow up with vinyl, under-thirty-fives feel a connection to the broader cultural nostalgia for the 1960s, 1970s, 1980s and 1990s, and the cultural values attached to these decades. Each have their own distinctive characteristics, unlike the blurring of decades in the current century. Is this a "pre-digital" phenomenon? It seems so, at least in part. Critically, for the album, the music of these decades is tethered to the format. The latter half of the twentieth century was the album era, and as the perpetual nostalgia for these decades continues, so does the association with the era's classic albums. Vinyl, in particular, feels like a tangible link to a golden age of music — when music wasn't just "consumed" but cherished. Young people are curious about a mystical time their parents have talked about before the iPhone, apps, streams and AI. A time in which a record was something beautiful and tangible to hold and not a soulless digital transaction. A time in which the analogue sound of a record was warmer and richer, in contrast to the compressed sound of digital music. Gen Z are sharing a love of music with mum and dad, going to gigs and festivals together and bonding over the same artists in a way Boomers and Gen Xers never did with their parents.

There is a very contemporary aspect to the trend for vinyl that is symbiotic with social media. Vinyl albums have become a symbol of cultural and musical taste, with Instagram, TikTok and YouTube amplifying the vinyl trend within the broader frame of "aesthetic culture". For younger audiences brought up on thumbnail images, the size and tactile quality of the record cover plays a major role in the appeal of vinyl. Hence, plenty of vinyl purchases are in fact never played, but simply lie in waiting for a time when the real-life environment can come somewhere close to the ideal vinyl luxury lifestyle displayed conspicuously all over Instagram.

Music industry consultant Patrick Clifton spotted this trend early as an underlying driver of the demand for vinyl in younger audiences. In August 2023, Clifton posted on Substack:

> "A focus on the sonic aesthetic—the quality and perceived loudness of the pressing, an absence of surface noise, etc—has been a critical feature of vinyl consumption historically, but a change in focus away from sound quality to visual features, from packaging to the vinyl itself is now evident among newer consumers of the format".

Clifton uses the example of Blood Records to make his point. The London-based company manufactures vinyl limited-edition runs of titles by major artists in striking visual variants, from unique marble and splatter though to zoetrope and picture-disc versions. Despite a compromised sonic quality when compared with classic 180-gram pure black vinyl pressings, Blood Records regularly sells out of these releases.

A study by The Vinyl Alliance reported that, in 2024,

> [on] Instagram alone there are over 39 million posts related to vinyl records, with youth sharing videos of their 'vinyl hauls,' turntables spinning favourite purchases, and walls decorated with colourful disks and sleeves.

Vinyl influencers @dadsdiscdelights (Zoë Timmers), @ stevekouta (Steve Kouta) and others draw huge audiences on

Instagram. Another super-spreader of "aesthetic culture" is Netflix, with many of its original series prominently featuring characters interacting with vinyl records. Examples include the sensational teen drama ***Euphoria***, cult German tech-horror *Cassandra* and, more directly focused on music, dramas such as hip-hop series *The Get Down*, Spanish drama *45 rpm* and Italian series *Mixed by Erry*. Most of all, the monster hit *Stranger Things* — whose 1980s setting is central to the show's cult appeal — features scenes of characters playing vinyl records in each of its first three seasons, which, if anything, somewhat downplays vinyl's dwindling status during that era. But why would a cult hit show feature someone slotting a CD into a tray?

No one predicted the vinyl revival; it just happened. Moreover, no one can explain it. Michael Kurtz, co-founder of Record Store Day, was quoted in *Why Vinyl Matters* thus:

> There was always a culture, and love, of vinyl before Record Store Day. In the first year or two, most of the people that came out to celebrate Record Store Day were in their forties and fifties. Now it's mostly people under twenty-five.

When Kurtz founded Record Store Day, he didn't anticipate the initiative's success either. Kurtz had previously run the Department of Record Stores and, together with other independent store owners and a supportive email from Sir Paul McCartney, he rounded up the Coalition of Independent Music Stores and the Alliance of Music Stores (you cannot accuse US independent record shops of lacking in collectives) to make these various networks of record stores more than the sum of their parts, at least for a day.

Metallica took up the mantle to help Kurtz and his band of indie store owners get the initiative off the ground with the world's first Record Store Day exclusive: not an album but a humble 7-inch single of live versions of "Jump in the Fire" and "Seek and Destroy". The band launched the event with an in-store appearance at Rasputin Music in San Francisco. All this was before the vinyl boom as we have come to know it. Metallica blazed the trail, and the following year, Jesse Hughes of Eagles of Death Metal started what would become a wildly successful artist "Ambassador" programme that has included Josh Homme (Queens of the Stone Age), Ozzy Osbourne, Iggy Pop, Jack White (appointed first "Global Ambassador" for 2013), Chuck D (Public Enemy), Paul Weller, Noel Gallagher, Dave Grohl, St. Vincent, Run the Jewels, Pearl Jam, Brandi Carlile, Taylor Swift and rock band Paramore. For the 2025 event, Post Malone has taken the role of Global Ambassador, and Sam Fender that of UK Ambassador.

Independent record stores see massive business spikes on Record Store Day, sometimes equating to a month's worth of sales in a single day. The event has steadily grown in stature, to the point of becoming a genuine global community. Record stores in over forty countries participate with live performances, artist signings and in-store events.

While the hypergrowth in social media platforms in the twenty-first century has been centred on the building of global "communities", there is indeed a true sense of community among vinyl shoppers. It isn't networked or monetised via an app, and it isn't obsessed with engagement. The community is remote but real, connected by the common behaviours of flicking through covers, random chat with record store staffers, the serendipitous joy of discovering a forgotten classic or something totally unexpected. A record store is both local and yet global, and the growing return of independent record stores around the world has as much to do with harnessing communities as Facebook, TikTok or Instagram or any other tech platform.

Record Store Day 2025, and I am back at Banquet Records. It's 4pm and there is still a ten-metre queue and a twenty-minute wait to get in. In the line behind me are two young male adolescents. They are "totally down" for Record Store Day, anticipating their haul. Maybe the Oasis singles box set, maybe the Sam Fender EP. But they are really here for A Tribe Called Quest's *The Low End Theory* (it's a coloured vinyl with a green and red splatter pattern, theirs for a mere £40). Their conversation then turns to the critical issue of when they are going to get a record player.

How long the vinyl resurgence will last is unclear, especially with prices for new releases and premium catalogue titles like *The Low End Theory* hitting the shelves at £30 or £40. The rising cost of materials is one thing, but it does appear that the music industry may be milking the vinyl market — a dangerous tactic that would see the industry repeating previous mistakes. Vinyl sales in the UK were down slightly in the first half of 2025, despite the typical boost received via Record Store Day. It means that vinyl growth can't be taken for granted, but the music industry has ignored such warnings in the past. One thing the music business has in its favour, however, is an across-the-board increase in music's cultural value, driven by the aforementioned group of female superstar artists. It opens the door for the music business to innovate on the album once again. But can it?

Chapter 5
Music consumption in the song economy

If the album has made a comeback both as cultural good and a music industry unit of supply, it still begs the question: Who's really listening? If artists are placing as much importance as ever on albums, and see making them as one of their ultimate creative goals, who are they really making albums for? There is no doubt that, in the streaming era, music consumers appear to have moved on — possibly a decade ago.

Or are listeners coming back around to the album? The British singer-songwriter Tom Odell, widely regarded a successor to any number of legendary troubadours seated at the piano, told me recently, "The cultural importance of music and artists is rising again, above the value of just songs". I feel like if anyone would know this, it is Tom Odell, himself an increasingly accomplished album artist. When it comes to new music trends coming over the hill, I would take the artists' instincts over "the industry's" every time.

The International Federation of the Phonographic Industry (IFPI) researches music fans' time spent consuming music, reporting its findings in "*Engaging With Music*: A unique snapshot of how fans around the world — over 43,000 in 26 countries — discover, listen to, and engage with [...] music". In 2023, consumers spent 20.7 hours per week listening to music (up from 20.1 hours the previous year — if you can believe the accuracy of those numbers). The report breaks down a list of some forty different activities people do while listening to music, claiming that, "on average, people engage in eight different activities while listening to music (rising to 12 among 16-24 year olds)". Presumably, this does not mean eight to twelve simultaneous activities (though that may be a glimpse of the future of human attention spans), but rather some subset of all forty, undertaken over a reasonable duration of time. Just one of the forty activities measured in the IFPI research relates to focused listening, and that is "relaxing and unwinding", with two in five people saying they do this as part of their personal mix of those activities. The message is clear enough: that music is mostly an accompaniment rather than the sole form entertainment for the vast majority of consumers — a strength for music in some ways, but a weakness in others. Music's ability to drop into the background while people do other things expands the opportunities for the music industry to monetise the "soundtrack to people's lives" — probably what the IFPI is driving at by putting a positive spin on the research. The music business has been very savvy about this, especially through the growth of streaming platforms but also in building solid commercial structures around music licensing to the providers of other forms of entertainment — and, more recently, to the providers of just about every other form of service. However, at the centre of this commodification has been the song, not the album.

The more music has been moulded by streaming to drop seamlessly into the background, the more people have become accustomed to that as the status quo. While we may be listening to ever-increasing amounts of music (I don't expect the IFPI will ever report the numbers falling), this raises some questions: who is still listening to albums? If anyone is, how are they doing it? And does it even really matter to the music business?

Let's take those questions in turn. First, who is still listening to albums? There's no real way to find out. Since streaming services don't disclose whole-album streams, a variety of old-school consumer surveys — rather clumsy attempts to capture behaviours as innate as "consuming music" — are the best we can come up with. A 2020 study released by Deezer, a rival streaming service to Spotify (and therefore, presumably, in possession of actual listening data), reported that just 9% of surveyed adults preferred listening to albums, with only just over one third of these claiming to listen to albums in sequence order. The numbers are, of course, skewed — this being a self-reported observation by Deezer users, who are bound to lean into streaming habits. However, they do get the point across — that focused album listening has become less common in the streaming era. Just over half of those in the Deezer survey said they listened to fewer albums than they did five to ten years ago.

Album listening has been on the slide, but does that mean music fans place less value on the album format? The US-based music research agency Music Watch looks to specifically measure the importance placed on albums by consumers who purchase music (via physical products and/or premium subscriptions). I like this question because it asks about attitudes, which surveys can capture better than real behaviours. From a study conducted among US music buyers in November 2024, 64% agreed (either strongly, or somewhat) that "the experience of listening to an entire album is important to me". Surprisingly, the response was even stronger in the younger generations, with Gen Z's at 68% and Millennials at 67%. Again, surveys are imperfect measures here, but the gist of the findings from these studies suggest a dichotomy — while only a minority of music fans are listening to albums, the majority still feel that it's important to them to do so, even when they don't do it. The IFPI study also reported that 13% of music consumers said they purchased a CD in the last month, while 9% purchased vinyl. Those numbers sound high, but even so, buying physical music is at best a niche activity, confined to a small minority. But listening behaviours get even more fractured. Fans' top reasons for buying vary, with 24% stating they like collecting vinyl records, 22% saying they like physically owning music, but just 19% saying they enjoy the ritual of playing a record and having the physical artefact to look at. In short, those who listen to albums in full are a fraction of a small minority of music fans. But does it matter?

As we enter the second quarter of the twenty-first century, it appears that the album is still valued as a cultural good, while it retains its importance in the music supply chain. If this breaks down at the point of "consumption", and we can't really measure that anyway, then it might not matter at all. At the height of playlist culture, it looked as if the album was in for some sort of reckoning, but that moment passed — a false alarm. Now it is playlists that seem distinctly passé. Tom Odell's theory, that it is music and artists that people care about above single songs, holds water. And that bodes well for the album, whatever the industry statistics say or don't say.

An album intends to put the music buyer, fan or even streaming "user" solidly in the realm of focused listening. That doesn't mean it can't work elegantly as background music, but listening that way misses the essence. As attention fades in and out, the listener will inevitably miss critical parts of the album journey. The subtle energy of the flow (carefully orchestrated by the scheduling of the tracks) goes unnoticed. If you are listening on vinyl, you may experience not noticing the end of side A as the needle glides around the inner grooves, just idling, until you snap out of it and get up to turn it over.

As a background experience, the album isn't a perfect fit, but as focused listening has reduced, "lean-back" or background listening has taken its place. Indeed, this passive form of listening seems to be the juggernaut powering the music industry through a decade of double-digit growth. Spotify has achieved what traditional retailers could not – it has made even the most casual music fans daily listeners and, via their subscription payments, passive buyers. The album as a body of work fits nowhere in this plan, and yet the streaming boom has revived the music business. This is how playlists became the most valuable real estate on streaming platforms. It no longer mattered whether the listener could name the song or the artist, so long as the track somehow found its way into the passive stream, with playlists and algorithm-powered streaming "radio" far outweighing album playbacks.

The booming song economy expanded into something way more than just playlists, however. It became the growth engine of the new music business both on streaming platforms and just about everywhere else music is played. It's why labels and publishers began staffing up their sync teams around the world. To score a sync in a movie or Netflix show is the new way to break a song — whether that song is new or decades old. A powerful sync places a song into a context that brings it right back into the cultural zeitgeist. The song then goes onto playlists and — bingo! — the money rolls in. Music legend Kate Bush acknowledged that her song "Running Up That Hill" was "given a whole new lease of life" thanks to the now iconic scene in episode four, season four of *Stranger Things*. To those in the music industry, this is simply another example of a very familiar narrative: classic songs of yesteryear being rejuvenated through placement in a modern cultural context. Kate Bush joined the ranks of Fleetwood Mac (a TikTok by Dogface208), Phil Collins (a YouTube reaction video by TwinsthenewTrend), Elton John (a remix single featuring Dua Lipa) and many other "legacy acts" who have enjoyed a gold-rush renaissance for their catalogues. Songs can be mined from the past and catapulted into popularity in an instant.

There is no better example than the Journey song "Don't Stop Believin'". It was originally released as the second single from the album *Escape* in 1981 (a fabulous album, as it happens). It was a modest US chart hit at the time (No. 9 on the Billboard Hot 100). Fast forward twenty-eight years to 2009, when the track had two very prominent syncs: *The Sopranos* finale and *Glee* (the song featured in six episodes). From there, the song ascended into the ranks of global popular culture. In 2009, it reentered the Billboard Hot 100, this time peaking at No. 4 and finally became a UK Top 10 hit, following several renditions on The X Factor. However, it is on streaming platforms where the song truly ballooned, steadily working its way into Spotify's Billions Club — the songs that have crossed the one billion streams threshold on the platform. The Billions Club has a rolling Spotify playlist (as at publication, over one thousand songs have now achieved a Spotify Billions Club plaque — and yes, there is an actual plaque). "Don't Stop Believin'" has since surpassed two billion streams.

As a consequence of this booming song economy, publishing and songwriter catalogues are being acquired at multiples of between ten to twenty times annual royalty revenues from streaming, radio and other use licenses. Hence that Queen catalogue acquisition by Sony Music at the handsome price of £1 billion. Songs in popular culture are helping to keep music competing in the "attention economy" — jostling with TV, games, books, spoken word, sports and now social media and "user generated content" for precious minutes of our time. The song economy makes hit songs more important than they have ever been. That's why, according to New York-based Hit Songs Deconstructed (which does indeed deconstruct the elements that make a major hit song, so that others can do their best to emulate that success) has been reporting a steady rise in the number of songwriters per hit. In the year 2000, the average number of songwriters per Billboard Top 10 hit was 2.4. This has increased to four in 2020. In 2024, over half of the songs to reach the Billboard Top 10 had at least four songwriters.

All this from songs extracted from their albums like diamonds from the rough. However, the sheer scale of major tech and social platforms is such that even if a tiny fragment of the audience are curious enough to explore where those songs came from, the halo effect can be significant for classic albums. The success of "Running Up that Hill" created a halo around its host album, *Hounds of Love*, which shortly after climbed to No. 12 on the Billboard 200 — its highest-ever US album chart position. The album became a big vinyl seller in 2022 and re-entered multiple international charts, including in Ireland, Australia, Canada, and Germany. A similar impact was felt with Fleetwood Mac's "Dreams" and the band's classic album *Rumours* — now a perennial best seller.

Perhaps however, those big classic albums are a protected species. The same cannot be said for the album format in general. As the major streaming and social platforms focus relentlessly on the engagement model, their algorithms serve a variety of stuff that encourages a sort of comfortably numb state of submission — ironically, a somewhat less engaged state that albums don't fit well with.

In complying with the growth of the song economy, it might be argued that the music labels have neglected the album. The jury is out on this one. Independent labels would never agree. But by staying album focused, they have been working against the grain of the song economy — and steadily losing market share as a result. Major labels, meanwhile, have almost certainly focused on songs (and marketed artists as celebrities) at the expense of albums. It's a trade-off they had to make to go along with the times. Record labels have limited resources and a lot of music throughput to take to market. There's no wonder they can't linger attentively on an album that isn't showing almost instant commercial promise — and most albums don't.

Catalogue departments, meanwhile, do very much focus on albums, but mostly those that have already proved successful. The easy money is in rereleasing classic albums and the back catalogues of legacy bands in new and ever more elaborate packages. The Super Deluxe Edition website is a constant flow of sumptuous reissues that make the "fifty-quid bloke" want to take out a second mortgage. But deluxe-edition album reissues are for a small niche of superfans and wealthy record collectors. Instead, in the new mass-market world of playlists, viral videos, the song economy and perfect-fit content, the album has not fared well. The more attention spans are fragmented across a constant feed of clips, the harder it is for people to spend forty minutes focusing on an album, even just once. And yet, albums work best when listened to repeatedly, potentially ***hundreds*** of times.

With the growth of passive listening, premium tracks by commercial music artists could also be swapped out for much more functional production music or copycat pop songs made by jobbing musicians on a salary equivalent. In Liz Pelly's book *Mood Machine*, she reveals details of Spotify's "Perfect Fit Content programme" (PFC), a fairly hideous scheme to take song substitution to extremes in the name of reducing content costs. Through PFC, Spotify paid production companies to create cheap, generic music by "ghost artists" in order to populate Spotify's playlists and reduce royalty pay-outs to real artists. Spotify acknowledges the existence of the Perfect Fit Content programme but denies that it is trying to increase the share of streams of Perfect Fit Content. It suggests that while songs were the gemstones of the music industry boom, they could in some instances be replaced with "fake songs", and in the context of lean-back playlists, the idea is that nobody would notice enough to care. But Spotify pays far lower prices for the content and therefore sees the tactic as a route to greater profits.

In a blog post in early 2025, the MIDiA Research music analyst Olivia Jones wrote that:

> As algorithmic playlists grow in popularity, listeners are becoming more comfortable with having music as background noise in their daily lives. As consumer behaviour evolves, the strategy of replacing licenced 'easy-listening' music with tracks commissioned in-house for a lower fee makes financial sense for companies like Spotify. This replacement would prove to be more profitable for the streaming platforms in the short-term but may end up driving away the dedicated music-listening culture that the platforms were originally built upon. If this happens, where does that ecosystem go?

Spotify's insatiable appetite for growth and world domination by way of controlling users' musical tastes has led to the inevitable: music generated by artificial intelligence rather than real artists. The most profitable songs of all on streaming services are those not created by human beings at all, but manufactured in the lab by AI models trained on millions of real songs. At the time of writing, in a written challenge to the UK government's proposed copyright reforms, Sony Music revealed that it has already requested the removal of more than seventy-five thousand AI-generated "deepfakes" of its artists' content from various networks on the web.

But a backlash has begun. The motivation of younger audiences in buying vinyl (and CD and cassette) has been to step away from the claustrophobia of connected devices to experience something more tangible, something requiring a committed choice, even an element of risk. In his book *How Music Works*, David Byrne writes that the main impression of digital music on the culture has been that people are now "seduced by convenience", with music streaming services the ultimate endgame — a destination where we can expect to find and hear any song ever made with a few thumb clicks. *Convenience* is certainly a driving watchword of the tech world (along with that other good one, *frictionless*). But why must everything be made so damn easy? So much so that we forget to care about anything?

As with all technology-driven trends, there is a contrarian response — a counter-trend in the form of a direct step into a more physical world, where entertainment and the appreciation of art require effort from the receiver. Whether it's a live gig, a trip to the cinema, searching the house to locate that book we are reading, or indeed, to pick a record off the shelf, take it out of the sleeve and drop the needle on the record, these are all experiences that demand active participation. The physical, mechanical activities involved reflect the effort required to earn some utility from it. There is also an important element of physical care we need to take with vinyl: to take care not to scratch the record, occasionally clean the record and, every so often, go to the trouble of replacing the tonearm needle. It's possible we do these things reluctantly but willingly, knowing it is all part of the equation. Contrary to living in a frictionless world, some degree of friction is the point.

But if we are going to go to the trouble of seeking out an album, reserving the time it demands to pay attention to it and the repeated occasions required to build a relationship with it, albums had better be good enough to offer a payback. As entertainment, in a world crammed with content and fragmented attention spans, how do albums still stack up?

Chapter 6
Classic albums then and now

March 2025, London's famous Royal Albert Hall. The band Bear's Den (a modern indie-folk outfit very much not from the Glasgow hinterland of Bearsden) are celebrating the tenth anniversary of their debut album, *Islands*, released in 2014. The show is in two parts, the second half a run-through of the album from start to finish. Chances are you are not familiar with Bear's Den, nor the album. *Islands* reached the lofty heights of No. 49 on the UK album charts the year of its release. Yet the 5,200-capacity venue is sold out. How? Bear's Den does music the modern way. Their brand of tender, emotive and inoffensive folk-pop has built a steady following through syncs on television shows and songs on major streaming playlists. The band bring a polished and restrained quality to their live shows. A couple of the songs from *Islands* are steadily cantering towards one hundred million streams on Spotify, where the band has 1.2 million monthly listeners. In a market where there is too much choice for pop stars to become a household name, the best a band can hope to achieve is to be a well-kept secret to a loyal fan following, while picking up a few streaming hits along the way. And Bear's Den are one of the lucky bands who find themselves in that category (two subsequent albums reached the UK Top 10). We may not know the album or care much about it, but to their fans, *Islands* is their *classic* album, deserving of a special evening and a celebration. It's as close as a modern band can get to joining the great canon of music works laid down in album form.

In September, I will see Welsh rock band Feeder do something similar with their own classic album, *Comfort In Sound.* Released in 2002, this album was a Top 10 UK hit and is a firm fan favourite — though, again, it never achieved mainstream success. The 2025 shows celebrate the album's reissue on vinyl and in an expanded version on CD and streaming platforms. It's the second time around the band has chosen to play the album in full in a live setting, the first time being in 2018. Whoever first thought of performing whole albums live was inspired. The idea has stuck, making album anniversaries perfect excuses to hit the road again, provided bands are happy to play old songs, some of them for the first time. It has provided another way for artists and fans to collaborate in keeping the album relevant despite whatever the digital tech bros have been coding up in the meantime. But to earn the capital to play an album right through in a live setting, doesn't it have to be a classic?

With the album's reduced commercial clout and its declining role in consumption, a dilemma crops up for all those involved in the endeavour of making one. Put simply: why bother? Why toil (sometimes for years) on a body of work that distils a hundred song ideas into ten tracks, spending a fortune in the process, only to see it flash across the charts and then evaporate into the mesh of a hundred million songs? It's an existential question for artists. Ricky Ross of the Scottish band Deacon Blue, told *The Art of Longevity* podcast:

> It's sort of madness, really, when all the good songs and books have already been written. Who wants to hear what's in my head or what we've

> created as a band? Does anyone even sit down and listen to an album now? But I think of it in the same way as poets, novelists and filmmakers. It's still worth doing if you feel you can do it well.

Albums remain key milestones for artists, each one an important body of work that, as a whole, come to represent the artist's career more than any other expression of their work. Indeed, in many cases it remains the pinnacle of an aspiring or emerging artist's ambition to get to the point of actually making just one long-playing record. If their career was to come to a grinding halt there and then, well, at least that important milestone was reached and a legacy has been left. More importantly, artists also know that albums are where great songs are born. As the artist Valerie June told me:

> If I think about an album, it gives me more of a soundscape to share moods and feelings and thought forms. An album to a song is a book to an essay, having more pages, having so much more space to move through. More pages and more chapters to create the body of work for me.

Sitting down to write one song isn't as likely a route to a hit as sitting down to write a body of work. A hit song has to be picked out of the chocolate box. Hit songs are taken from the album. Then the hit leads listeners to the album and drives the deeper connection that transforms the listener into the fan. That's why all those "song driven" projects during the iTunes era failed to deliver anything of note. The song and the album work in symbiosis — as Jack Antonoff recognised: "A single without a great album is a long hallway that leads to nothing."

But artists don't just want to make an album as a destination for the song. They want to make the album as a journey for the listener. As such, for the album creator, the process of creation of that journey is more like putting together a puzzle, or indeed mapping the journey; the album as a creative quest.

An artist's true desire, however, is to make a *classic* album — a definitive contribution to the scene and an entry into the music history books. A classic album cements an artist's long-term cultural impact and demonstrates a depth beyond hit songs. On *The Art of Longevity*, I have asked many artists the question: "What's best for longevity — a hit single or a classic album?" Without exception, artists answer that a classic album matters more. There is little doubt that many bands of longevity are motivated by albums rather than hit songs — Jack Antonoff was right about that. Indeed, plenty of established artists have made classic albums without a single hit on them. Fiona Apple's *Fetch The Bolt Cutters*, Solange's *A Seat at the Table* and Radiohead's *A Moon Shaped Pool* are a few examples from recent years.

But what makes a classic album in the modern music business? The answer is much more nuanced than it used to be. In the pre-digital era, classic albums were judged by a combination of actual sales (not the made-up streaming equivalents), cultural impact and long-term influence. High chart positions, months (not weeks) on the charts, critical reviews and plenty of ongoing press would combine to generate a word of mouth that would send an album into the annals of music history, to be much quoted by other artists and frequently included on "all-time" or best-of lists. In other words, not forgotten about. Some albums transcend the usual criteria altogether and enter into a sort of mystical reverence. I feel this way about Love's *Forever Changes*. In Tim Burgess's

Vinyl Adventures from Istanbul to San Francisco, Burgess thinks that *Forever Changes* became album folklore:

> It guaranteed its enduring status not from radio plays but from older siblings who would pass it down through what they saw as their responsibility for the musical education of their brothers and sisters. Almost impossible to emulate, it stood up alongside *Sgt. Pepper* and *Pet Sounds* as the stone tablets of what could be achieved with an album.

Released in 1967, *Forever Changes* was inducted into the Grammy Hall of Fame in 2008. On its 2020 list of the 500 Greatest Albums of All Time, *Rolling Stone* ranked it No. 180. It's hard to think of an album being capable of that kind of slow-burning legend today, but its continued influence suggests that artists still see it as something to aspire to.

A combination of tangible, measurable commercial achievement and cultural impact could once make a classic album pretty much inarguable. According to our scholar of the long-playing record, David Hepworth, the last true classic — as classified by the above measures — was Michael Jackson's *Thriller*, released in November 1982. In his words, *Thriller* is to albums "where this story ends". Others, such as academic Tim Footman, author of *Radiohead – Welcome to the Machine: OK Computer and the Death of the Classic Album*, categorically points to *OK Computer* (1997):

> a record that seemed to encapsulate its time and yet still seems as resonant and relevant today. Radiohead are rare in that they have balanced critical and commercial success for many years,

> and their most famous offering exemplifies that achievement, enduring analysis at the fingertips of academics even as it exists as background music in coffee bars.

If we can say that a classic album today still requires a trinity of commercial success, cultural impact and longevity, the way we measure these factors has changed. Viral moments and social media influence can give an album brief exposure, but it's a flash in the pan. A big push for chart success can also make an album peak faster commercially, but after that, so little is known about how much the record is really listened to and in what context. Mostly, even the really good albums seem to quickly evaporate from our consciousness.

A classic album in the "post-album" age of streaming is hard to define and probably impossible to nail down. This is probably why Tim Footman regarded *OK Computer* as the last time an album counted as a bona fide classic — an album that reflected society and was widely discussed and celebrated in its long-form. A record that very much characterised a decade. Over a quarter of a century on, it feels like we have descended into a culture that tries to circumvent or avoid these collective moments — a culture in which we allow technology to flatten depth, reduce communal feeling and fragment shared cultural experiences — certainly in terms of music. In 2025, it was a TV show — the Netflix drama *Adolescence* — that seemed to have succeeded in creating a shared national experience of the kind that was more common in the era of broadcast media. Could an album have this effect now?

Two factors have combined to destroy the monster successes of the album's imperial past. Firstly, unit sales — as previously examined — only truly exist in the physical realm, a small fraction of the industry's value. While the format can only generate a modest minority of industry revenues, record labels cannot afford to truly prioritise albums. The bigger problem, however, is the sheer weight of volume. Although no official number is tracked, the number of album releases has almost certainly increased year-on-year since streaming hit hypergrowth in 2015. By this measure, of course, the album is anything but dead. The problem is there are just too many for us to dwell on one long enough to make it a classic.

With stream counts nailed squarely onto individual songs (at least the first thirty seconds) and no reports of album consumption in existence, commercial metrics are all but redundant. A classic album might now simply be defined as one that is listened to a lot by many people, but we won't know unless Spotify decides to tell us which albums made the grade. As we've seen, chart success is simply now the byproduct of a numbers game, with even a coveted No. 1 reduced to the status of a promotional badge.

In which case, a classic album must come down to the second measure — that of cultural impact. But this is a debate, of course. One person's classic is another's dud. Only very occasionally do critical reviews, industry awards and actual consumption all line up to break an album into the wider cultural consciousness. In recent years, we might pick out Taylor Swift, Billie Eilish, Beyoncé or Kendrick Lamar as having success in this respect. It used to be that consulting a trusted media brand such as *Pitchfork*, *Rolling Stone* or the *New York Times* would guide us towards the best albums released in any given year. These lists would contain the same fifty records, but in a different order. But today, each list from each outlet varies massively. Each is a dizzying display of albums you have not heard by bands you do not know and will never have the time for. There really is just too much music.

Perhaps the personal perspective is more valid these days. With algorithms feeding us more highly personalised content and albums in such plentiful supply, the idea of agreeing on what makes an album stand out from the rest seems a pointless exercise. After all, music isn't a competition. A more subtle evaluation would relate to how we personally enjoy the journey of an album and how it qualifies as something special to us. Albums that:

- take you on a listening journey through the scheduling of the songs from beginning to end, ebbing and flowing in energy across their duration;
- you would not consider listening to an individual song from, out of context from the others;
- improve with repeated listening, revealing new depths and hidden stories and sounds;
- you look forward to hearing again with excitement, but you will delay the experience until the right time and context comes around so that you can indeed focus on it;
- continually reveal the individual songs as something that rise above and become your favourite for a time, until another one takes over;
- transcend boredom, commanding you to play them over and over for years and years. If an all-time classic, you will play it through at least once a year and may return to it for repeated listens at some point in later life.

Through any of the above, we begin to form a relationship with albums in a way we cannot with songs, or with any other form of art for that matter. We think of them as friends, largely because we spend a lot of time with them and hear them frequently. As Travis Elborough writes in *The Long-Player Goodbye*:

> Who hasn't thought of songs on a particular album as a set of companions, at some time or other? And LPs can be rather like friends. We fall out with them. We grow up and move on. We lose contact and find new ones. And then, years on, renew our acquaintance, only then remembering why we fell for them in the first place.

I certainly have this relationship with any number of albums, often from my formative years: *Zenyatta Mondatta* by The Police, *Bad Reputation* by Thin Lizzy, *Skylarking* by XTC, *Scoundrel Days* by Aha. In the case of *Zenyatta Mondatta*, my original acquaintance was such a powerful experience that the bond "between us" is exactly that of an old friendship. I discovered the album on my doorstep, on a chilly winter's night in 1980. I heard a knock on the door and a motorbike speeding away down the street. I went down the stairs, opened the door, stuck my head out and looked around. Nothing — just cold, still air and the sound of that motorbike speeding off into the distance, two or three streets away by now. Then I looked down, and there it was on the doorstep — an LP record. The sunset burst in the background and the band's three headshots in that distinctive blue triangle, with The Police logo set at an angle and the words "*Zenyatta Mondatta*" in an Eastern scribe. Egyptian, was that the effect? Exotic for sure. What did (does) *Zenyatta Mondatta* even mean? It's one of my favourite band album covers (which is what makes the

Spotify canvas for "Don't Stand So Close To Me" so cool). I took it upstairs and put it on the turntable. I was excited to hear it, and up until that point, I hadn't spent much time with albums. I was twelve years old. Albums were like the musical equivalent of watching a live football match in real time — they took too long. But listen I did, over and over and over again. In 2024, I bought a copy of *Zenyatta Mondatta* as a Christmas present to myself. I needed it in the collection. I've played it a dozen times and thoroughly enjoyed it. I must have heard this record two or three hundred times. It isn't even my favourite Police album, and it certainly isn't any of The Police's favourite either. The common wisdom is that *Zenyatta Mondatta* was a rush job, containing two instrumentals and more than a few inconsequential filler tracks such as "Canary in a Coalmine" and "Man in a Suitcase", as well as an extended "jam" called "Shadows in the Rain". But, just as our duty as loyal friends is to accept our friends as they are, flaws and all, without judgement, there isn't a moment on that record I do not love, and despite the passing of thirty-six years, I have never got bored of it.

I'm not the only fan of this record. So too, apparently, is Joni Mitchell. Her first album of the 1980s was *Wild Things Run Fast*, on which her voice was gravelled with a smoking-induced husky quality, and her songwriting was both more experimental and political — and it had "big drums". *Wild Things* was her eleventh studio album, the first (of five) on which she collaborated with bassist Larry Klein, whom she married that same year. Joni stated that her influences for the album included Steely Dan, Talking Heads and, in particular, The Police. She said of the latter, "The sound of the drums was one of the main calls out to me to make a more rhythmic album." That must have been nice for Sting to hear, given that, by this time, his main complaint was of the overly complicated, showy drumming style of genius percussionist bandmate Stewart Copeland. Take that, Sting!

Since we're on the topic of Joni Mitchell, it is Joni who may well have made the classic album of all classic albums. Certainly, *Blue* is a favourite album of many, including many of her fellow musicians. The album's mystique is most beautifully described in Ann Powers's Mitchell memoir, *Travelling*:

> The songs remain in the present tense in which they were created. Maybe it's impossible to know what happened when Joni Mitchell made *Blue* because every time the record plays, it's still happening.[12]

Perhaps Mitchell qualifies as the ultimate album artist. Each of her nineteen original studio long-players (I'm including *Both Sides Now* and *Travelogue* in that count, for purists) is different from the previous one — each epic in nature and each containing a centrepiece that anchors the records firmly in classic territory. I can certainly say this about the records she made *before* she became obsessed with The Police single "De Do Do Do, De Da Da Da" (another Ann Powers reference) in 1980. And yet, all of her albums combined produced just one hit single: "Help Me" from 1973's *Court and Spark* (while "Big Yellow Taxi" from *Ladies of the Canyon* was also a minor hit in the UK). Mitchell's procession of albums represents an artist continually progressing, even after the ultimate creative peak of *Blue*. And yet, the album that best represents Mitchell's peak

---

12 *Travelling: On the Path of Joni Mitchell*, by Ann Powers, Harper Collins, p. 191.

is up for debate. Fans and admirers may make their choice from any one of half a dozen or more different titles. While her later albums have not aged particularly well, the ten she released before 1980 continue to accrue cultural value. They always will. The only thing I can suggest to the uninitiated is that Joni Mitchell records are best played at nighttime. The later the hour, the deeper the dimension they seem to take on.

There is always a special place for those albums you love, even if you are not particularly a fan of the artist. When my wife first introduced me to *Raintown* by Scottish band Deacon Blue, I wasn't immediately convinced until she quite rightly insisted I play it a few times. I came to love it. The album is often celebrated as one of the most fully formed debuts ever. I can't say I love any other Deacon Blue albums, but *Raintown* stands on its own as an astonishing creative achievement. Themes of growing up, work, money and dreams make *Raintown* as universal a concept as any record, and yet it is fundamentally its quality as a musical tribute to Glasgow that most Scots are proud of.

These examples and my above criteria draw on personal experience, however. With the charts forever changed and much less relevant today, perhaps the opportunity is for the music industry's award makers to step into the role of credible cultural authority on those albums that deserve our attention. But who are they to judge, anyway? Most awards are designed to celebrate mainstream success — to make nominees and winners the talk of the town — yet in the streaming era "the mainstream" has itself become just another niche. Awards are still trotted out by the music and mainstream press as a way of benchmarking stars and, in particular, distinguishing superstars from the rest of the pack. Whether it be introductions to media interviews or blurb on the sleeves of books, summing up how many major awards a star has racked up is an effective shorthand for validating both popularity and talent. Awards are very much part of the establishment, but their influence and prestige seems to be on the wane, in line with the general demise of mainstream media. But music industry award shows could do better for artists and the album in particular. They are the only high-profile convention of both legendary artists and new artists that are breaking into the realms of stardom. That has to count for something. New artists aspire to join the pantheon, but to do that, they have to have a good enough run to make their best work. To have their work recognised at the level at which they enter into the realm of the great and the good is as meaningful as it gets in today's business. The validation is hugely important to artists.

Chapter 7
The future of the album

In a conversation I had with a UK major record label boss, sometime in 2023, I was told, "Artists still want to make albums, but we don't really know what to do with albums any more." It's a serious dilemma for record labels. Their new signings and emerging artists still want to make albums, while their established bands and superstar artists don't know anything different and are not going to change the habit of a lifetime.

In May 2024, Spotify CEO Daniel Ek famously tweeted: "Today, with the cost of creating content being close to zero, people can share an incredible amount of content."

It was one Ek's many transgressions on the subject of making music. Albums are in fact expensive and time-consuming to create; each represents a significant investment of capital for those financing the project — in the case of many established and legacy artists, it is the artist themselves laying out the cash. An album of any real quality, even one recorded in an artist's home studio, is likely to cost upwards of $50,000. But a priority album released by a record label may run up costs of half a million or more. Either way, far from zero. But, with ninety-nine thousand songs uploaded onto streaming platforms every day,[13] not to mention AI generated

[13] Luminate's "2024 Year-End Music Report".

tracks and versions now flowing onto those services, precious few albums now cut through the clutter to connect with the culture in the way that will get the project anywhere close to break-even, never mind profitable. In this scenario, labels are forced to cut their losses and quickly move on from an album that isn't showing early promise. It's a dilemma, because in the streaming era, even the best albums take time to build a head of steam. In recent years, some of the most commercially successful albums, including Chappell Roan's *The Rise and Fall of a Midwest Princess,* Noah Khan's *Stick Season,* Sabrina Carpenter's *Short N' Sweet,* and most famously, Charli XCX's *Brat*, were not immediate successes. Instead, these records took hold steadily as singles blew up, social media buzz scaled and the artists toured relentlessly. These records slow-burned their way to becoming "event albums". This is in contrast to the days when new albums by superstar bands were guaranteed to make a splash. I often feel that this state of affairs must mystify the great and the good of the artist community: those who have made numerous classic albums in the past and sold millions upon millions. Bruce Springsteen has had a long and successful relationship with Columbia Records, dating back to his 1970's debut, *Greetings from Asbury Park, N.J.* Their partnership has lasted decades, producing numerous iconic albums and a dozen Billboard No. 1 albums, including all-time classics such as *Born In The U.S.A.* and *Tunnel Of Love.* But can you name the title of The Boss's latest album of new material?

It was called *Letter to You*, released in October 2020, Springsteen's twentieth studio album of original songs and his first with the E Street Band since 2014's *High Hopes. Letter to You*, inevitably awash with themes of aging and death as its creator entered his eighth decade, was met with widespread critical acclaim and was, by modern standards, a success, topping several international sales charts. It is a remarkable achievement for Springsteen to still be putting out high-quality albums, with relatively little filler, after fifty years. The album is one of Springsteen's most successful records this century. It was certified Gold in Germany and the UK and was Springsteen's twenty-first Top 10 album in the USA. Other than that, *Letter To You* has evaporated through music's ozone layer. The most streamed track on the album on Spotify is the title track, with twenty-four million streams. Not insignificant, even for the world's 314th (gulp!) ranked artist on the platform. Yet the song isn't quite 2.5% of the stream count of Springsteen's biggest hit "Dancing in the Dark". There is almost nothing that Bruce, or his record label Columbia records, can do about this. It is simply down to the times we live in. As David Hepworth wrote in his essay "Memo to Our Old Favourites: It's Not You, It's Us":

> No new record by Donald Fagen, Bruce Springsteen or Tom Petty or anyone else that was making records back in the seventies and eighties is ever going to be listened to as intently as the record that made their names.[14]

It's not you, Bruce; it's us. Columbia Records put a lot of effort into promoting *Letter to You*, pulling all of the typical marketing levers for a major album release: several lead singles, trade marketing with streaming services, press events and behind-the-scenes content. Springsteen himself was involved in the campaign and was excited about the album and its re-

14 *Nothing Is Real*, David Hepworth, p. 147.

ception. But I imagine that, on some level, he is ambivalent. For Springsteen, releasing an album kicks off a new cycle of a much more vital and rewarding activity, namely hitting the road (although in this particular case, COVID-19 made touring impossible). Touring is where an artist of Bruce Springsteen's status can still make proper money, while enjoying the visceral connection with his devoted audiences.

But Columbia Record's job is to make money from the recordings, so how did it fare with *Letter To You*? That's a whole lot more complicated. While the album profit and loss account might not look anything like healthy (certainly when compared with his classics), the "business model" for music albums has become more complex in the streaming age. At the time of the album's release, Springsteen was still one of Colombia's most important artists, even after fifty years. A year after the release of *Letter To You*, however, he became a whole lot more important, when the label's parent company, Sony Music, acquired his entire song catalogue in a deal worth $500 million. The deal embraced both his recorded catalogue and his songwriting, transferring Springsteen's royalties from both to Sony. From now on, a key objective of any new album campaign for Bruce Springsteen will include reigniting interest in his back catalogue, every single stream of which will make money for Sony. As for Springsteen, his only objective, one assumes, is to keep on creating music, because that is what he does. Perhaps, though, like many other established artists, Springsteen no longer needs to crank out original albums in the old way. His twenty-first studio album, *Only the Strong Survive*, was a covers album of classic soul songs from the 1960s and 1970s. In the summer of 2025, Columbia announced that it would be releasing no less than seven "new" Bruce Springsteen albums — all of old songs. *Tracks*

II: The Lost Albums is a truly massive box set, featuring seven complete LPs that Springsteen recorded between 1983 and 2018, but then left in the vaults. In recent years, Springsteen has placed creative energy into making films and innovating his live performance work. A few years before, *Springsteen on Broadway* broke new ground for the legend in a way a new album never could. The concert residency first held at the Walter Kerr Theatre and St. James Theatre in New York City ran and ran — in the end for over a year. A Netflix special and soundtrack album were significant successes. For legacy artists, the balance has tipped in favour of working the legacy material harder rather than attempting to add to it.

Let's take another example, and what better example here than the world's most ambitious band, Coldplay? Here, we are in higher stakes territory than even Bruce Springsteen, since at the time of writing, Coldplay occupied the sixth spot in Spotify's ongoing artists world ranking (gulp again, for different reasons). Coldplay is the sole band in the Top 10, by the way, illustrating how the power in music has swung heavily towards solo acts. Their tenth studio album *Moon Music* was released in October 2024 by Parlophone in the UK (as with Bruce, the band has been with its major-label partner since their debut, *Parachutes*, in 2000) and Atlantic Records in the US. Unlike Bruce, Coldplay is highly likely to want to move on to be an independent band. The album is the second chapter of their *Music of the Spheres* trilogy, the first being *From Earth with Love* (2021). Being one of the world's biggest bands automatically qualifies a new Coldplay album as a major "event release", and the fanfare around this release was something extraordinary, with meticulous planning, intricate marketing tactics and an exceptional budget. No less than three editions of the album were released: *Notebook*, *Tour* and

Full Moon. Each one came with exclusive content, including voice memos, live sets and bonus tracks.

Moon Music went down like a lead balloon with critics, but critical reviews do not stand in the way of a band like Coldplay. In their unstoppable bid to remain the world's biggest band, Coldplay has tapped cool artists of the moment as collaborators (including Beyoncé, Rihanna and that well-known injection of street cred, The Chainsmokers), a tactic that has paid off massively. On *From Earth with Love* they included BTS and Selena Gomez. For *Moon Music*, the band turned to UK hip-hop (Little Simz) and Afrobeats (Burna Boy) to give the album a concentrated dose of relevance. Pop-up listening parties, a Record Store Day collaboration in the USA, and the obligatory appearance on *Saturday Night Live* pump-primed the album's first week sales — enough to see the album debut on the Billboard chart at No. 1. Still, it didn't seem like enough. Coldplay were so keen to get momentum behind *Moon Music*, Chris Martin and his bandmates turned up on the QVC home shopping channel to promote it, along with hawking a range of related products that included a toaster and tea set, based on the album artwork. The irony was not lost on Chris Martin, who explained: "Because we're older now, we're moving into crockery and Tupperware. The music is really just serving our kitchen line now."

As context to all this, Martin had previously hinted that *Moon Music* could be the band's final album. This has been rumbled as a classic Coldplay tactic — an attempt to make their new record a scarce item in an abundant world. Since *Viva la Vida or Death and All His Friends* (2008), Chris Martin has been threatening to end the band's career or take them into the hibernation of a hiatus. The band's *A Head Full of Dreams* (2025) was also "the end of something". As part of

Moon Music's release, Martin was more definitive, insisting now that the band would finish after twelve albums — just two more to go. He told Apple Radio's Zane Lowe:

> Having that limit means that the quality control is so high right now, and for a song to make it, it's almost impossible, which is great. And so where we could be kind of coasting, we're trying to improve.

A modest vinyl collection (photo by the author)

These examples are used to make the point that — even as music becomes more and more abundant — an album release does not become any less effort, cheaper to make, or more optimal in any way. It is simply much less likely to be memorable. Of course, budgets aren't what they used to be. Michael Jackson's rumoured $30 million budget for *Invincible* in 2001 represented the last of the big spenders, but the biggest priority albums released by major labels can still hit the $1 million mark. Hence record label tactics to make their priority releases some kind of cultural event. The problem is that, despite their best efforts, new albums come and go in the blink of an eye. Since label marketers know this all too well, the album release isn't usually seen as the start of something, but an endgame. The album campaign is designed to build as much buzz around a record as possible, and focus all efforts and budget to achieve the highest possible chart position at the week of release, and then swiftly move on, job done.

This is all fine, but hardly justifies the artist's labour on a record. An album is a year or two (or more) in the making. Often, fifty or even one hundred demos and song ideas are whittled down to a final selection. Writing and studio recording time become obsessively demanding for the artist. On *The Art of Longevity* podcast, Jeremiah Fraites of the American duo The Lumineers said: "Even to make one song is impossible. It's so much work. One song is already a pain in the ass, before you talk about doing a full LP."

After the songs are finally complete, it's into the scheduling, which many artists also obsess over. In the vinyl boom, artwork, liner notes and packaging are other major considerations — so much so for some artists that they are as important as the music. When it's all done, there is a waiting game of between three and nine months while the record label gets its ducks in a row to put the record on the market. The artist is then pushed into a condensed schedule of promo appearances: radio and podcast interviews, press and blog interviews and, in Coldplay's case, manning the phones in a call centre. After two years of work and waiting, the album has about two to three weeks to make an impact on the world. By this time, the artist is already working on new material, and the cycle begins again.

Of course, there are rare exceptions to the "evaporating LP", and these, thankfully, still exist — not because of humongous marketing budgets but because they connect in the way art has a unique ability to do. This happened in 2024 by way of the "*Brat* summer". English singer-songwriter Charli XCX had been working her way into the consciousness of pop culture through the course of five previous albums, numerous collaborations and most notably, by the summer of 2023, some major festival appearances. But still, she was in no way a mainstream artist or household name. By the following summer, everything would change. And it was her sixth studio album, *Brat*, that changed it. It's safe to say that this album, influenced by the 2000s British rave scene, hit a cultural nerve. The best thing about it is that nobody understands exactly why. This didn't stop the theorists. Zoe Williams, writing in the *Guardian*, explained it: "Charli XCX's new album, *Brat*, highlights how many young women currently aspire to live — dirty, hedonistic, happy and bra-less. Well, it beats journaling after a long day of pilates."

Of course, for starters, *Brat* was not just good, but consistently great. According to Metacritic, which compiles scores from music critics, *Brat* is the highest-rated album of 2024 (and the sixteenth-highest-rated ever). The album was shortlisted for the Mercury Prize for 2024 Album of the Year, which signalled how the industry cognoscenti could rally around a pop record, sensing a reason to celebrate the format — and create some much-needed street cred for those awards in the process, perhaps? Once the album had caught on in Europe, another minor miracle happened — something increasingly rare for UK artists — *Brat* broke Charli XCX in America. The album was nominated for nine Grammy Awards at the 67th annual ceremony, including album of the year. It ended up winning in the best dance/electronic music album category instead. *Brat* charted (No. 3) in the USA and, as previously stated, then won a BRIT Award.

As with Coldplay's *Moon Music*, the album was injected with momentum by way of further editions. A deluxe edition, *Brat and It's the Same but There's Three More Songs So It's Not*, and a remix album, *Brat and It's Completely Different but Also Still Brat*, featuring twenty guest artists. Unlike *Moon Music*, these albums took on a life of their own, further propelling *Brat* to a widening audience. It became that rare thing in today's content-saturated world: impossible to ignore, a genuine talking point. As with classic albums of old, there was more to *Brat* than the music. The cover art came in a contrarian lime green with cheap, pixelated font, becoming a social media meme. It was infamously (unsuccessfully) adopted by Vice President Kamala Harris's 2024 presidential campaign after Charli XCX tweeted in her favour.

Brat is the kind of success that gives the music business an almighty lift in confidence. When these moments happen, the industry rallies round, sensing a reason to believe. *Brat* wasn't a front-loaded album campaign, but a genuine surprise phenomenon, a snowball that turned into an avalanche. It didn't even make No. 1 in the UK album chart, peaking at No. 2. But unlike those heat-seeker-missile chart albums that just need to hit No. 1 for a day, *Brat* didn't stop selling. And it didn't stop streaming, staying on the chart for months rather than weeks. Of course, a surprise success is different from an accidental one, and *Brat* was no accident. It was a well-crafted and meticulously detailed piece of work — in the songwriting, production and packaging — even that rough artwork was carefully thought out. If you want to succeed in the music business, it all takes work, and nobody knows that better than Charli XCX. In a TikTok post, Charli XCX addressed fans thus:

"I've been thinking about BRAT long before the record coming out. I've sat here for two years prior, thinking about how I'm gonna communicate this record to the world. Not just the music but the whole visual identity of the album".

She planned it all and it worked. But what about the majority of artists looking to carve out a living and a career through making records? For a clue, here's a music quiz question: which album narrowly beat *Brat* to make the top of *Pitchfork*'s best of list for 2024?

It was Cindy Lee's *Diamond Jubilee*. *Pitchfork* described the album thus:

> The 32-track magnum opus from the glamorous alter-ego of Canadian musician Patrick Flegel hit the scene like some old movie where a mysterious drifter shows up with their guitar to breathe new life into a sleepy town. Presented as a two-hour listening gauntlet with no breaks between tracks—or as a sketchy download link on a GeoCities website that channelled Heaven's Gate—*Diamond Jubilee* seemed to float in from another place and time.

That's not the only remarkable thing about the *Diamond Jubilee*. Patrick Flegel has consistently rejected streaming platforms in favour of physical and limited-access releases. Cindy Lee releases are often on physical formats only, or available to download on Bandcamp instead of streaming services. Also in 2024, Jack White surprised fans by distributing his new album, *No Name* (his best work in a long time), exclusively on 12-inch white vinyl records, given away for free with (qualifying) purchases at his own independent record shop, Third Man Records, located in Detroit, London and Nashville. The album was held off streaming and digital platforms for two months. For now, these are unusual examples, but both albums were — by most measures, other than stream counts and chart position — successful. While the idea of holding off from releasing albums on streaming platforms seems counterintuitive, physical only releases might become an attractive option for independent artists who now sadly realise they are making virtually no income from streaming.

March 2025. I am being shown around the "factory" of Elastic Stage by its founder and CEO, Steve Rhodes. Founded in 2016 but funded by a substantial investment in 2023, the London-based company specialises in on-demand vinyl and CD manufacturing for music creators and labels. Rhodes has built a platform that enables artists to produce and distribute physical music formats without upfront costs or lead times. An artist at any career stage can decide to print and sell just ten vinyl records through Elastic Stage (provided they own all the copyrights). Rhodes is an enigmatic, larger-than-life character. He is the author of a trilogy of books on human design, a science that "decodes the energetic wiring of the human body", but in a past life, he was a pop star. In fact, he was the "Austrian George Michael", briefly signed to CBS Records. There is no doubting Rhodes's enthusiasm for design, technology, vinyl, or music. "I like big machines," he says, beaming at me enthusiastically, as a robot that looks like something out of *The Terminator* cuts another bespoke album record (Elastic Stage claims to manufacture vinyl with a quality equal to that of a major traditional pressing plant).

But if an artist sells a vinyl album for £30 through Elastic Stage, they are likely to see about £20 in profit, approximately ten times the return for making a traditional vinyl record through a label. The idea is to allow even emerging artists to achieve their ambition to see a record produced in physical form (vinyl or CD) and to make decent money from it (provided the record sells, of course). Rhodes envisages the project to be the scale of a streaming platform, solving the limited capacity for making vinyl records and, especially, opening up that privilege to creators at all career stages. And if it does work, the album may return to the kind of physical volume sales last seen in the twentieth century. It's hard to tell if Rhodes and his company exist in a parallel universe, but if so, it's a utopia for artists that represents the opposite of Spotify.

So far, Elastic Stage has seen little enthusiasm from the record labels, however. As ever was, the music industry's infrastructure lags behind technology and consumer trends, not least when it comes to albums. Ironically, the industry's inertia in this respect may be key to the album's survival. As new technologies such as downloads and streaming have emerged as threats to the industry status quo, music companies have simply thrown up a protective shield — a combination of copyright laws and an oligopolistic grip on industry structure — and slowly adjusted themselves into a position of advantage. In the case of digital music, the recording industry has built back up to its peak CD revenues over a two decade period, but now with added profitability and a perpetuity model for monetising deep catalogue. It has done so through a combination of legal enforcement, dogged negotiation and a somewhat risk-averse licensing strategy. In the LP and CD eras, if music fans wanted to listen to one of Queen's old albums, they would simply pick it off the shelf and put the record on. The music industry made no further money from the transaction. In the streaming era, when we hit play on an old Queen song, the industry collects real cash.

This license to print money for music catalogues has never been in better shape. In 2024, music economist Will Page measured the value of music copyright at $45.5 billion per year — that's just the recorded music and publishing annual revenues from music sales and licences. The new boom in the wider music economy is bigger than the peak of the CD years of the 1980s and 1990s. No wonder global superstars like Sting, Bob Dylan and Bruce Springsteen decided to cash in their chips and sell off their songwriter copyrights to global investment funds and music companies. The music industry has seen a return to growth in the streaming music era, with investment pouring into music and music tech, launching hundreds of new start-ups — all of it fuelled by the increase in songs being released by music artists at all stages, from aspiring young wannabes to established legacy artists who have been making music for half a century. It is songs that are at the centre of this model rather than albums.

The music industry's stubborn resistance to let go of the album is all the more remarkable because it has not been the result of a co-ordinated or concerted strategic effort. There have been industry initiatives, but many of these were launched tentatively. Take National Album Day. The UK music industry initiative was launched in 2018 by the British Phonographic Industry (BPI) and the Entertainment Retailers Association (ERA) in partnership with BBC Music and the backing of other industry organisations, primarily major and indie labels. It was created to celebrate the album format and its cultural significance. I recall a lunch with Geoff Taylor, then CEO of the BPI, a few days before the launch, and he was in a pensive mood. The launch event was taking place at YouTube's music hub in London, the usual press launch and speaker panel affair, and Geoff wasn't sure how the industry establishment was going to come across launching a celebration of an outdated format, of all places, within the four walls of YouTube. After all, YouTube was a colossus of digital music, an album-crushing sledgehammer. I sympathised but could offer little by way of encouragement. Or ideas. The prevailing mood in 2018 was that the album was perilously close to irrelevance, an anachronism. Worse, it was something of a stalking horse for anyone working on the tech platform side of the music business. No streaming platform was going to lean into the album. Who in their right mind would spend such a huge chunk of their precious time - forty minutes - listening to an album?

As it turned out, doubts were unfounded. The launch of National Album Day in 2018 was a modest but considered success. It received strong industry support from artists, record labels and music retailers, especially independent record stores, who marshalled their scant resources around the idea with local events across the UK. The initiative gained significant media coverage, particularly BBC 6 Music, a bastion of music culture and the album (and itself a survivor of a near-death experience when Director General Mark Thomson announced the service was to be cut in 2010).

Perhaps the album was still something to recognise and even celebrate. That inaugural National Album Day focused on celebrating seventy years of the album, marking the anniversary of the LP format. The positive reception led to National Album Day becoming an annual event in October, six months apart from the now well-established and qualified success of Record Store Day, held each April. National Album Day builds on new themes each year, which have included famous albums by female artists, the 1980s, the 1990s and subsequently 1990s classic albums by British bands. In 2025 the event focused on Rock albums. Each year, the event has grown in size and significance, with high-profile artist ambassadors like Noel Gallagher, Lewis Capaldi, Kylie Minogue and Elbow adding credibility to proceedings, even to the point of giving a modest boost to sales. The initiative has played a part in the album's steady ascendancy in the 2020s and has helped reassert the music industry's confidence in the format — at least in the UK. A long way from its tentative beginnings, it's surprising that other countries have yet to adopt the idea, especially considering the global success of the companion event Record Store Day.

In other parts of the music industry ecosystem, inertia has kept the album on life support. The Album of the Year Grammy is still the biggest award of that ceremony, the equivalent of Best Picture at the Oscars. Yet music industry awards are clearly going through an identity crisis. Several high-profile artists, including The Weeknd and country star Zach Bryan, declined to submit their work for consideration in any category for the 2025 awards ceremony, and it seems like more will follow. Many artists do not want to comply with the idea of making music a competition. Similarly, the UK's previously credible and respected Mercury Music Prize, launched in 1992 to celebrate the best British albums each year, appears to have lost some of its initial kudos and promotional and career impact for the winners, dwindling to a small, unceremonious prize and lacking a headline sponsor in 2024. Meanwhile, the 2025 event shifted outside of London to Newcastle, partly because Newcastle's City Council put up the money to host it. No doubt the Grammys, Mercury Prize and other awards will grind it out, but it feels to me like there is a gap for another type of album-based prize — something that underpins the idea that classic albums are still being made. Whispers of a music award created by Spotify and Netflix together began circulating as this book was written, but based on previous form, I can't see albums featuring as a category.

Many in the music business predicted that streaming would weaken, even kill off the album format. The thinking was that, within the engagement model of streaming, artists would be better off releasing a constant flow of single tracks — in other words, a constant reminder to fans not to forget about them. In any case, listeners would no longer have the attention spans to cope with whole albums. Like a lot of things in today's polarised world, it's both true and yet not true.

A fabulous creation and still a beautiful thing

Contrary to expectations at the start of the century, the album is now a stronger format than ever. Albums remain the currency of the physical music business, which, driven by the vinyl resurgence, is now making such a recovery that, in some markets, vinyl is the fastest-growing music format. Remarkably, this is being reflected by music fans, who have returned to buying vinyl records in their droves, even if only half of vinyl buyers actually own a turntable. Owning the vinyl LP has become an expression of fandom and a symbol of support for the artist.

Ultimately, one of the hidden pleasures of vinyl is that personal choice wins out over the terrifying abundance of music streaming. While it's hard to argue with the sheer value of paying £12.99 a month for access to almost every song in history, the self-imposed scarcity of paying double that for one LP record is oddly liberating. This scarcity used to be imposed on us. In the previous century, if we wanted to hear a record, we would have to go and look for it, then put money down to acquire our very own copy. We'd then need to get it home on the bus and play it. None of this was ever something to complain about, but part of the actual joy of it all. No wonder we miss it so much that recreating the routine seems worth it, at least on occasion. If you are a music fan and have the means — and the time — it seems that more and more new music choices deserve to be vinyl purchases. After all, didn't the creators involved in making that music put blood, sweat and tears into its production?

But I do think that our current, renewed love for vinyl is complex. Many of the ideas we have about vinyl are essentially fantasy. We *imagine* a utopian scenario in which we can be at home, with no distractions and no one else around, so the volume can be suitably high. We *imagine* having a spare forty minutes or perhaps even an hour — enough for a proper listening session. We *imagine* choosing a suitable title — a recent purchase, a new release or perhaps a classic, and then commencing the ritual: taking the record out of the sleeve, dropping the needle, etc. Just put the record on, kick back on the sofa and simply listen. The reality is entirely different, of course. The number of times we get to enjoy listening in this way is like waiting for a month full of Sundays.

It's a guilt trip, sometimes — playing vinyl records, or attempting to. With listening time so scarce, it is inevitable that our vinyl collections far outweigh the time we spend playing them. In 2025, I bought about forty titles, and I do wonder how much more playing time about thirty-five of these will get. In truth, I'm still waiting for the perfect opportunity to listen to the Waterboys' new double album, *Life, Death and Dennis Hopper*. Opportunities to play four consecutive sides of vinyl really are few and far between.

The rarity of the vinyl listening experience seems at odds with the idea of making vinyl purchases of new albums a habitual thing. Besides, it is expensive. At £30 a pop, and requiring some effort to engage with by today's standard of digitised convenience, vinyl records come under the category of luxury product. The trend and the joy of vinyl is almost certainly conspicuous to some extent. Is it about having that stock of records on the shelf as decoration — a show of identity or just the promise of a more relaxed, culturally enriched, less distracted future? Is this why many people — especially younger buyers — have vinyl collections despite not actually owning a turntable? There is nothing quite so elegant as vinyl, certainly not from the perspective of music formats. The music and culture writer Stephan Kunze's *zensounds* blog puts it well:

> Do you realize that some of these artefacts are extremely beautiful? People spend much time and effort on designing sleeves, choosing materials and even hand-crafting limited vinyl, CD or tape runs in special boxes, putting together liner notes and credits. I always loved reading through booklets while listening to music.

Indeed, one look at the library of vinyl record covers designed by Hipgnosis (the design agency, not the music catalogue fund) makes you realise just how much of a cultural powerhouse the format once was. Despite my conflicts and doubts, the whole vinyl ritual seems worth buying into even if it is really more illusion than reality. Vinyl culture is complex, but that makes it all the more interesting. Albums are to music what cinema is to film, and what cocktails are to drinking. They bring a little decorum into your life.

Perhaps the answer is more discipline. Put the phone in the other room, or turn the damn thing off. Put routine listening sessions into the calendar — once a week would be a start. The rare times I have achieved true vinyl-to-sofa sessions in recent years have been so immensely enjoyable, I can't think of anything more beneficial to anyone who calls themselves a music fan. I am proud to call it a hobby. We live in an absurd way, in a mad world. When you jump on a train, who wouldn't want to enhance the experience of travelling by staring out of the window and playing Elliott Smith's *XO* on the headphones, or *High Violet* by The National, or any other one of a million plus albums that can soundtrack a journey like a work of art? Instead, we're scrolling socials, checking emails — or worse, watching TV (whoever watches TV shows on their phone on the way to work needs to reevaluate their life). It's engaging with nothing in particular and being distracted by anything at all. A good book, or a good album, can take you away from all that and literally bring you back to life by way of escaping from it.

Long may the album's commercial and cultural resurgence continue, but I hope we can do it justice by placing enough priority on our time to really enjoy albums as we used to. Let the long player be a life hack. And if you have a collection but no turntable, then start saving up now and buy one good enough to do the format justice. You will never look back.

I've finished this book now, so I'm opening that Waterboys concept album *Life, Death and Dennis Hopper*. I'm hoping that, for the next 40 minutes or so, nobody asks me for anything, no one notifies me of anything or god forbid comes to the door. On the inside of the gatefold sleeve is a note from Mike Scott, lead singer of the Waterboys and orchestrator in chief of this magnificent project. It says:

> The album is chronological. The songs can be listened to in any order and stand as discrete entities independent of the tracklist, and videos for certain songs can be found online, but the record is designed not to be shuffled or watched, but heard as a full programme. Experienced as such it becomes a soundtrack to a unique film that will play on the screen of your own imagination.

Here we go then Mike…

Afterword

Celebrating the album

"Fortress album"

Twenty-five titles that have helped the format survive the twenty-first century

As the twenty-first century arrived and digital music swept across the music business, many believed the album's days were numbered. You could say the writing was so clearly written on the wall — the album's obituary writers outnumbered the believers. But these titles, among many others, eventually proved them wrong. It's merely a list, mostly of albums you will know something of, even if you didn't become familiar with them at the time. Whatever your music tastes and your predilections about the artists, you will find something to enjoy here — or at the very least, admire. My criteria are qualitative — each of these records achieved a combination of commercial success, cultural impact and subsequent importance to the music industry and, in turn, preserved the relevance of the album format. As such, these choices are, at the very least, great examples of cohesive song collections — i.e., a unified body of work. These albums go down as modern classics, if you will — albums of significance at the time and still influential now. Of course, you will have your own list. I encourage you to share, along with your reasons, which you can do on my website: songsommelier.com

2000

Radiohead, *Kid A*

Not only the album that brought back experimental rock, but a self-correcting, left-turn follow-up to the band's monster success, *OK Computer* (defined by some as the last true classic album). *Kid A* was self-sabotage but was so good that people saw through it. The songs may have been messed with by technology and made weird with sound effects, but they were still great songs. The subsequent success experienced by the band was of a different flavour to the typical music industry recipe. No attachment to expectations, no obligation, no pressure - other than that which they placed upon themselves. *Kid A* made every other artist want Radiohead's career: uncompromisingly creative and commercially successful, while tearing up the music industry playbook. Moreover, *Kid A* was a true body of work.

2001

Jay-Z, *The Blueprint*

The Blueprint dropped on 9/11. The album remoulded the sound of modern hip-hop, thanks in part to production (Kanye West and Just Blaze). With 4.5 million copies sold worldwide, it cemented Jay-Z's legacy, but wasn't put on streaming platforms until October 2015. *The Blueprint* proved that the hip-hop album was in fine health as the age of digital music took hold.

2002

Norah Jones, *Come Away With Me*

Selling over thirty million copies worldwide, *Come Away With Me* restored faith among record labels that they could still have massive hit albums, even as Napster and file-sharing tore through the industry like a wildfire. Record label bosses wanted Norah Jones to speak out against file sharing, but she preferred to get on with the job of making music. It was one of the most successful jazz/pop crossover albums ever, propelling Jones onto a long career as a major artist, even if the record became something of an albatross, given her desire to experiment and transcend music genres.

2003
Evanescence, *Fallen*
Amy Lee's songs were essentially piano ballads retooled into radio-friendly pop-metal anthems. It was a manufactured concept, not without risk, but it worked. The album brought "emo" into the mainstream, with anthems like "Bring Me to Life" and "My Immortal" helping the album sell seventeen million copies worldwide — even at the height of file-sharing and as the music business hit the skids. Bringing a young frontwoman into the fading "nu" metal scene also worked. It's easy to forget just how massive it was at the time, and *Fallen* has aged surprisingly well.

2004
Green Day, *American Idiot*
Shifting sixteen million copies worldwide, this was to become the last rock album to achieve a global cultural moment until probably Arctic Monkeys' return with *AM* in 2013. A comment on the post-9/11 era, "Boulevard of Broken Dreams" and "Wake Me Up When September Ends" became anthems that made Green Day momentarily the biggest band in the

world, and who would have thought that was possible on hearing the band's debut, *39/Smooth*?

2005

Mariah Carey, *The Emancipation of Mimi*

Liza Minelli said that a career in show business is essentially a series of comebacks. Selling over ten million copies worldwide, album number ten was a massive comeback for Mariah Carey, and "We Belong Together" became one of the biggest hits of the decade. Where she might have faded into insignificance, this album reestablished her as a dominant pop and R&B force. These days, she is pop royalty, so much so that she doesn't "do stairs", apparently.

2006

Arctic Monkeys, *Whatever People Say I Am, That's What I'm Not*

Described by *Rolling Stone* as "a start-to-finish rush of invigorating riffs and pointed narratives that heightens with repeated exposure", which says it all. It proved so much: that guitar music could be reinvented, that a provincial British rock band could be sensationally good, that an indie label could launch a massive hit band even as the music industry tanked. One of those albums that you love more the more you listen. A blistering debut that launched an enviable career.

2007

Amy Winehouse, *Back to Black*

A modern soul masterpiece, this was an album in the old-fashioned style. It was so authentically retro that it was hard to believe it was contemporary. It sounded more like something from your parents original record collection. Winning five Grammys and selling twelve million, it (controversially) elevated Winehouse to the status of pop icon and arguably began to put female solo artists on a pedestal — though the consequences for Winehouse, and some others, were tragic. Built to last as a body of work at a time when the album was becoming genuinely threatened, it also had a generation of artists looking back in order to move forward.

2008
Kanye West, *808s & Heartbreak*
With brazen use of auto-tune and minimalist production, this was an album of provocative and bewildering hip-hop, pop and R&B all at once. Songs like "Heartless" and "Love Lockdown" were the beginning of a more personal and vulnerable era for superstars that influenced an entire generation of artists. Albums that risk everything but then do actually work can end up going down as classics, whether you like them or not.

2009
Drake, *So Far Gone*
By releasing a mixtape, Drake rekindled interest in the long-form record — i.e., the album — at a critical time. Unlike traditional DJ-hosted mixtapes, this project had album-like cohesion, original production and high-quality mixing. It was one of the first projects to blow up via blogs, MySpace and

early streaming platforms, showing the power of digital distribution before streaming was to become the norm.

2010

Kanye West, *My Beautiful Dark Twisted Fantasy*

Pitchfork: "Bearing witness to Kanye West's very public 2010 has featured many joys, none greater than watching everyone unspool his myriad updates, achievements, and indiscretions into piles of meaning. His persona went to cataclysmic places this year — there were times when he deserved his own cable news ticker. But, somehow, West managed to transcend the preposterous talk show appearances, the too-good-to-be-true Twitter account, the live breakdowns, the Horus chain, the free-MP3 stunt(ing), the press blitz, the breakups, the make-ups, the dick pics, the furniture pornography, the Rosewood movement, the NO NEGATIVE BLOG VIEWING, the living paintings, the short film, and the rest of the lot. Through all that noise, we obsessed first and most deeply over the eye of the storm: the album."

2011

Adele, *21*

With sales of over thirty-one million copies worldwide, *21* was a cultural phenomenon that demonstrated that the music industry's good times may well be on the way back. Featuring hits like "Rolling in the Deep", "Someone Like You" and "Set Fire to the Rain", it was packed with modern classics and rightly transformed Adele into a global superstar.

2012

Lana Del Rey, *Born To Die*

Born to Die spent over five hundred weeks on the Billboard 200 and sold more than ten million copies. It launched Lana Del Rey into mainstream success, despite her music being uncompromisingly strange. With *Born To Die*, Del Rey fully formed her signature cinematic, melancholic and sepia Hollywood-inspired sound and aesthetic. All this set the Instagram and social media "sad girl" aesthetic culture into a frenzy. No wonder an army of infatuated girls (and some boys) all over the world became devoted fans. Del Rey continues to work solidly in album form, with each one a statement of intent as to where she wants to take her perfect brand of melancholy next.

2013

Lorde, *Pure Heroine*

With the hit single "Royals", Lorde became an international sensation, but the quality of *Pure Heroine* throughout signalled the arrival of a new talent and a different kind of pop star. The album's success marked a shift toward a more independent, alternative pop scene, and completely opened up the space for a wave of other great female solo artists. Lorde's success resonated with a generation that felt disillusioned by mainstream pop, and now there's no such thing.

2014

Beyoncé, *Beyoncé*

The surprise release of the album (December 2013) broke new ground in the music industry and showed how digital platforms could be turned to artists' advantage. Beyoncé's empowerment themes and visual album format made it a touchstone for pop music in 2014 and set the bar high for each and every subsequent Beyoncé album, with each one being a true cultural event. A glorious achievement in the digital age.

2015
Kendrick Lamar, *To Pimp a Butterfly*
Pitchfork: "It's an album by the greatest rapper of his generation, where his rap skills are perhaps the least noteworthy talking point. An album so dense with ideas that it made the novelistic turns of his debut—a thoughtful and textured, gang culture-adjacent coming-of-age story—seem quaint and straightforward by comparison. It's an album that is on this list not only because of its merits, but because it's presumably why so many albums are not here, this year—it's not a stretch to reason that To Pimp a Butterfly had something to do with why Kanye West and Drake didn't release proper studio albums in 2015. It's an album with such gravitas that the runaway success of Adele's 25 seems inconsequential. It's not just the album of the year; it's the voice of a moment in time."

2016
Solange, *A Seat at the Table*
This album was Solange's first chart-topping album, but the personal exploration of Black womanhood, resilience and self-care in the face of systemic oppression made it a classic album in the era of the Black Lives Matter movement. A concept album of sorts, on vinyl it was a double album. Creatively, the post-genre blend of neo-soul, R&B, funk and jazz,

with a dreamy, minimalist production style, created its own musical trend. The album made effective use of spoken-word interludes from Master P (and answerphone messages from Solange's parents) adding depth to the storytelling and, again, setting off a trend (though she wasn't the first to do it). It was featured in best albums of 2016 lists by publications like ***Pitchfork***, ***Rolling Stone*** and the ***New York Times***.

2017
Kendrick Lamar, ***Damn.***
Brimming with intellectual prowess and humour, ***Damn.*** was not just an album, it was a cultural statement. ***Damn.*** blends hip-hop, trap, R&B and soul with Kendrick's dexterous lyrical genius. The whole album is genuinely addictive, but tracks like "Humble.", "DNA.", and "Loyalty." became anthems, and the album's exploration of identity, race, faith and society resonated deeply — but also broadly, way beyond hip-hop fans. ***Damn.*** hit the sweet spot between cultural sensation and commercial success, winning Best Rap Album at the 2018 Grammys. Better still, it was awarded the Pulitzer Prize for Music, a historic achievement for hip-hop. Pulitzer said of ***Damn.***: "a virtuosic song collection unified by its vernacular authenticity and rhythmic dynamism that offers affecting vignettes capturing the complexity of modern African American life". How about that for a body of work?

2018
Kacey Musgraves, ***Golden Hour***
By the time 2018 rolled around, not only was the music industry booming again, but high-quality albums were back in plentiful

supply. While streaming had fuelled a huge boom in rap, hip-hop, pop and Latin genres, country music was now having its day too. *Golden Hour* was important because it did that rare thing that few records do — it crossed over. It infused elements of pop, folk, disco and gentle psychedelia, making it accessible to listeners beyond country and inviting them into the genre at the same time. The songwriting (and the production on the record, by the unique Daniel Tashian) is lush. It won a Grammy and swept the board at country music award shows, but *Golden Hour* also encouraged other artists to have a crack at country music.

2019
Billie Eilish, *When We All Fall Asleep, Where Do We Go?*
Eilish's debut was a commercial and cultural success. The album's dark, minimalist production, unique blend of electronic, pop and indie influences and Eilish's haunted vocals resonated with a wide audience. Hits like "bad guy" and "bury a friend" became global sensations, while the album's subjects of mental health, anxiety and self-reflection connected with the Gen Z prevailing themes. The album earned Eilish multiple Grammy wins, including Album of the Year, and solidified her as a new global icon in the music industry.

2020
Taylor Swift, *Folklore*
Swift's surprise "lockdown album" was a dramatic departure from her earlier pop sound, embracing a more indie-folk, alternative rock and indie-pop style. Released deep in the throes of the COVID-19 pandemic, the album received widespread critical acclaim for its

introspective lyrics and more stripped-back production. Songs such as "Cardigan", "Exile" (featuring Bon Iver) and "Betty" showed a more mature, reflective side of Swift. *Folklore* became a cultural phenomenon and was seen as one of the year's most significant albums, winning Album of the Year at the 2021 Grammy Awards.

2021
Adele, *30*
Released on 19 November 2021, it marked the return of the long-overdue album, coming nearly six years after *25*. It demonstrated that the album could be a highly anticipated global event. In the "always on" culture, Adele had done things the old way. She had gone away, got married, started a family and taken her sweet time to come back with another massive album. And, critically, it was the album in which she gave Spotify a good ticking off for its outrageous policy of setting automatic shuffle on album playback.

2022
Harry Styles, *Harry's House*
A game-changing album for Harry Styles, marking his evolution from boy band heartthrob to mainstream pop icon. The album combined elements of pop, rock, funk and indie, with standout tracks like "As It Was" and "Late Night Talking". If Styles fancies himself as a modern-day Bowie, with *Harry's House* he blended in some Cliff Richard and Leo Sayer just for fun. Styles's first interview for *Harry's House* was done for *Better Homes & Gardens*. Now that was how to launch an album in the music business of 2022!

2023
Bad Bunny, *Un Verano Sin Ti*
Though it was released in 2022, *Un Verano Sin Ti* continued its cultural march well into 2023. Bad Bunny's genre mash-up of reggaeton, salsa, trap and bachata not only dominated Latin markets but became a crossover phenomenon. It was also a streaming behemoth, breaking records for Latin artists worldwide. His follow-up leaned much more into tradition, proving him to be a real album artist.

2024
Charli XCX, *Brat*
Brat has influenced the pop landscape in 2024, reinforcing Charli XCX's status as a key figure in boundary-pushing, post-modernist pop and digital sound experimentation. Least likely of the bunch to be seen as an artist who could hold the torch for the album, she has turned out to be the leader of the pack.

2025
Wolf Alice, *The Clearing*
The London band had a huge amount riding on their fourth album, not least their transparent desire to break the US market. Whether *The Clearing* helps achieve that, it will not be for the lack of quality therein. The band can't make a bad song, and these 11 tracks hang together in the manner of a late-70s classic. I'm plumping for this album to endure and make its mark for one of Britain's best rock prospects.

Still hitting the heights

Great new albums by older bands

As mentioned, artists still map their careers in albums, not single songs. Many of the artists I've featured on *The Art of Longevity* podcast have very recently made superb albums, including Morcheeba, Travis, Tindersticks, David Gray, Mogwai, Rickie Lee Jones, Crowded House, Nerina Pallot, Turin Brakes, Everything Everything, Ed Harcourt, My Morning Jacket, Norah Jones and The Coral.

Bands from as far back as the 1980s are still making superb albums now. In 2024, The Cure famously returned after a sixteen-year absence from releasing new music with *Songs of a Lost World*. The album has a critic score of 90 (on the Album of the Year website), the highest in their entire catalogue. Users rated it at 84, the highest score since the band's 1991 classic *Disintegration*. Depeche Mode made arguably their best album since 1993's *Songs of Faith and Devotion* with 2023's *Memento Mori*. Another classic 1980s band, Orchestral Manoeuvres in the Dark, released a fine album, *Bauhaus Staircase*, in 2024. As singer Andy McCluskey told presenter Fenner Pearson on *The Art of Longevity*: "It's usually dangerous and stupid to make a new album unless you are really going to invest in it. People tell us we're iconic and influential, so we don't want to fuck it up by making a shit album." You can't say it better than that, and fuck it up they did not.

Some 1990s bands are doing even better. American indie band Nada Surf made one of their finest albums so far in 2024, with *Moon Mirror*, a record that has revived the career of this somewhat forgotten band. Consider Welsh indie rockers Manic Street Preachers. The Manics have had creative ups and downs, as is reasonable to expect for a band of thirty years. But their most recent two albums, *The Ultra Vivid Lament* (2021) and *Critical Thinking* (2025), are both superb late bloomers.

Most impressive of all, for me, are Suede, whose 2022 and 2025 albums, *Autofiction* and *Antidepressants*, their ninth and tenth studio records respectively, represent a creative peak for a band that has previously created classic albums. Like careers, albums ebb and flow, but there's nothing better than seeing a band at any career stage — whether it's the debut or album number twenty-five — make a fine record that they can be proud of as a body of work and an addition to their oeuvre, one that goes down well with critics, fans and new listeners alike, even if we can no longer say that they have made an undisputed classic.

Further Reading and Resources

Vinyl aspirations and inspirations

Here are some great books, websites, podcasts and live events I love, all about albums.

Books to read

Long Players: Writers on the Albums that Shaped Them (Bloomsbury). Tom Gatti compiles many of the Long Player editions that have been published in the *Spectator*.

A Fabulous Creation: How the LP Saved Our Lives (Black Swan) Music scholar and journalist David Hepworth on the album's imperious period, 1967–1982.

Why Vinyl Matters (ACC Art Books)
Jennifer Otter Bickerdike's passionate deep dive into vinyl, put together with great interviews with well-known and renowned artists, songwriters and other vinyl enthusiasts.

Lastly, not just one book about albums but a whole series. If you have yet to hear about or try the 33⅓ series of books (Bloomsbury), start now. Just pick your favourite record among those covered and get reading. Each book is readable in one sitting and, for many, you'll do just that. As series creator David Barker wrote about them:

> This series is based on the idea that when we fall in love, we want to immerse ourselves in the object of our love. We want to know the history, the backstory — and often, we want to know what other people think. Surely we can't be the only ones to feel this way about "Veronica Mars," about Jonathan Coe...or about Led Zeppelin IV?

My favourites are Warren Zanes on *Dusty In Memphis* and Annie Zaleski on Duran Duran's *Rio*.

Websites to sign up to

The Needle Drop
If you think album reviews are dead, think again. Anthony Fantano ("the internet's busiest music nerd") is a one-man album review machine, and his reviews go down a storm with a large audience of millennials and Gen Zer's who previously couldn't have cared less about critic reviews. Forget Rolling Stone, a thumbs up from this guy can set a record on the way to success.

Rate Your Music
Now here is a curious thing – an open source website straight outta the year 2000 (literally, it was launched that year). RYM is an "online encyclopaedia" of music and films, with millions of user album reviews and ratings (out of five). It

features theme and community-based charts for the highest-rated releases. It's more influential than official charts, and a lot more fun too.

Sound Matters
A comprehensive resource and community about vinyl, albums and sound quality, Sound Matters was created by music enthusiast and marketing professional Marc Henshall.

Auditory Musing's Daily Records
I've been following this curated site for a while now, and the album recommendations — eclectic as they are — reflect the impeccable taste of curator and clinical pathologist (yes, you read that bit right) Pulin Kothari, the Auditory Muser himself. Pulin has now recommended some 250 album titles, each and every one worth checking out.

Albumism
The features on this site will have you crate digging and enjoying the album in all its long-playing glory. It's just really very good indeed.

Ways to get out and listen

If you are finding it hard to set aside the time for a listening session at home, or perhaps you have yet to invest in a vinyl or high-fi music set-up, then check out three great ways to get out and listen to records in a focused and celebratory way:

Classic Album Sundays
Founded by DJ Colleen "Cosmo" Murphy way back in 2010

in a North London pub, with the intention of promoting enjoyment of true listening as the age of digital music began to take hold. According to the website, Classic Album Sundays "tells the stories behind the albums that have shaped our culture". It does so incredibly well.

Pitchblack Playback

Albums are meant to be an immersive, focused experience. The only distraction should be to get off the sofa and turn the record over. This is the ethos of Pitchblack Playback. The British curation and experience brand encourages music fans to "hear classic (and new) albums & exclusive pre-release premieres on powerful, immersive sound systems, in the dark". Listening to whole albums from start to finish in almost complete darkness is a refreshingly fun experience.

Music bars

Japanese jazz *kissaten* (old-school coffee shops playing jazz) became popular from the 1950s in Kyoto and Tokyo. It's taken a while, but the trend is finally catching on in the UK and other countries. London's House of Koko has beautiful vinyl listening booths, while bars like Brilliant Corners and Spiritland have dedicated listening events and always plays something interesting through high-end and vintage audio systems.

Your local record store

Independent record stores have been in steady resurgence for a few years now, thanks to vinyl and the trend for human experiences and owning and collecting records. Many will host listening parties, artist signings, intimate performances and special events for Record Store Day and National Album Day. What are you waiting for? Get down there!

Album podcasts

If you want an idea, I'd suggest starting a really good albums podcast. There are precious few good ones. The problem with most of them is that regular podcast hosts often talk about albums they don't actually know that well or even like much. What's the point of that? Others are way too nerdy, which is fine if you are into listening to nerds, but I'm guessing you have much better things to do. I've got two that I would recommend.

The Album Years
Musician Steven Wilson and co-host Tim Bowness delve into their favourite albums from a particular year, once again treading the boards of the album's golden years of the late 1960s through to the 1980s. Like a lot of album discussion, the commentary stops on anything released this century. It's a whistle-stop tour and refreshingly avoids music snobbery, while being very British. Sometimes it's clear that neither host really knows much about the albums they discuss — how could they? There are too many for that. But even when they breeze past something, it works perfectly well as a reminder to make an appointment to listen again.

Tim's Listening Party
The Charlatans singer, author and broadcaster Tim Burgess was bang on trend during the pandemic with his enormously popular *Tim's Twitter Listening Party* (now, ironically, on Absolute Radio and as a podcast). Although it's not quite as dynamic as a radio/podcast format as it was on Twitter, it's still a joy.

Also available from Repeater

Justify My Love: Sex, Subversion, & Music Video

Ryann Donnelly

In *Justify My Love*, Ryann Donnelly explores sex and gender in one of the most widely consumed art forms of our age — the music video.

Through an autobiographical reckoning with the author's life in a band and collaboration with past lovers, and a close analysis of the erotic iconography of music videos, *Justify My Love* tells the subversive history of this medium, from the inception of MTV in 1981 through to the 2010s.

Covering everything from Lady Gaga and Beyonce to Nine Inch Nails and George Michael, *Justify My Love* shows how subversion became mainstream, and how marginalised voices shaped some of the biggest music videos of the last thirty years.

Order online from RepeaterBooks.com

REPEATER BOOKS

is dedicated to the creation of a new reality. The landscape of twenty-first-century arts and letters is faded and inert, riven by fashionable cynicism, egotistical self-reference and a nostalgia for the recent past. Repeater intends to add its voice to those movements that wish to enter history and assert control over its currents, gathering together scattered and isolated voices with those who have already called for an escape from Capitalist Realism. Our desire is to publish in every sphere and genre, combining vigorous dissent and a pragmatic willingness to succeed where messianic abstraction and quiescent co-option have stalled: abstention is not an option: we are alive and we don't agree.